Your wellness
DIY

INSPIRING AND HEALTHY LIVING PRACTICES

DESSISLAVA DONCHEVA

BALBOA.PRESS
A DIVISION OF HAY HOUSE

Balboa Press books may be ordered through booksellers or by contacting:

Balboa Press
A Division of Hay House
1663 Liberty Drive
Bloomington, IN 47403
www.balboapress.com
844-682-1282

Because of the dynamic nature of the Internet, any web addresses or links contained in this book may have changed since publication and may no longer be valid. The views expressed in this work are solely those of the author and do not necessarily reflect the views of the publisher, and the publisher hereby disclaims any responsibility for them.

The author of this book does not dispense medical advice or prescribe the use of any technique as a form of treatment for physical, emotional, or medical problems without the advice of a physician, either directly or indirectly. The intent of the author is only to offer information of a general nature to help you in your quest for emotional and spiritual well-being. In the event you use any of the information in this book for yourself, which is your constitutional right, the author and the publisher assume no responsibility for your actions.

Any people depicted in stock imagery provided by Getty Images are models, and such images are being used for illustrative purposes only. Certain stock imagery © Getty Images.

Print information available on the last page.

ISBN: 979-8-7652-4650-4 (sc)
ISBN: 979-8-7652-4648-1 (hc)
ISBN: 979-8-7652-4649-8 (e)

Library of Congress Control Number: 2023919864

Balboa Press rev. date: 10/31/2023

I dedicate this book to all who feel lost, scared and anxious
but still believe that life has something more to offer!

CONTENTS

PREFACE

Dear reader, thank you for choosing this book from the sea of books. Perhaps something inside you has led you to pick it up, whispering that here you will find what you need. I believe this will be an important step towards taking control of your own life and it won't be an easy one, but I also know that together we can make some changes to help you deal with sadness, anxiety and fears. I say it because I've been through that myself, and every piece of advice in this book is based on my personal experience.

We live in dynamic times when, more than ever, we have to face thousands of challenges every day. Often, we are inundated with negative news, tasks that must be completed here and now, and expectations that need to be met. At work, we are constantly chasing deadlines, and at home, instead of the desired rest, we often have to juggle between household chores and taking care of our loved ones. When we are in good health, it's easy to handle the countless commitments, remaining calm and optimistic. However, this is extremely difficult when we are dealing with a health issue. Even the smallest change can then cost us enormous efforts, making us feel exhausted, desperate, tired and negative. And when we struggle with sadness, fears, anxiety, and negative thoughts, our lives easily turn into a joyless burden. We start feeling lost and doubtful about being healthy again and getting back the joy and love in our lives. I'm saying all this because I know from my personal experience what it's like to feel helpless and confused about which way to take.

For me, everything started in 2016 when, after a car accident (fortunately with no serious injuries) and with the accumulated stress from years of constant travelling and taking care of my little son plus the chronic neglect of self-care, I collapsed both mentally and physically. Looking back, I realize I had ignored the signals for a long time without taking the time to address them. As a result, the following two years brought me face-to-face with conditions unfamiliar to me until then — panic attacks, depression, fears, intrusive thoughts, and phobias —that made each day extremely difficult to endure. I entered one of the darkest periods of my life which, alongside my suffering, opened doors to new knowledge. We often hear that everything that happens to us has a reason and that the challenging moments help us grow the most. I have contemplated this a lot, and though I'm conscious of my growth, looking back, I can't help but feel saddened, remembering the darkness and pain I went through. At the same time, I know that though this period caught me off guard and shook me, I realized that life is not only sunshine and roses but there are also pain and difficult moments we can overcome with faith, effort and the right means. I learned that the most important thing in our lives is taking care of our own health, especially what we eat and drink, how much sleep and rest we get, how we relax and recharge our batteries, and what thoughts we allow to govern our consciousness.

I became aware of the fact that nowadays, many people are struggling daily to maintain their normal functioning and find light in their days filled with fear, sadness, and helplessness, desperately seeking help and support. The thought that I might be able to help some of them by sharing what I have learned motivated me to write this book. I know each person walks their own path, and sometimes all we need is a little support and guidance. So, I sincerely hope that this book will be one of the aids on your journey.

However, keep in mind that life is constantly changing, and nothing in it is permanent. Even the most unbearable state rarely lasts forever. Every effort is worthwhile, and step by step, we can change things.

With the right information, self-care and faith in success, you are also on the right path.

Often, in difficult moments, I find motivation in the thought that we cannot expect something new and different if we keep doing things the old way. My grandmother used to say: "This, too, shall pass," and whenever I remember her words, I feel stronger. When one seeks solutions and wants to cope with a situation, the Universe responds to their prayers and provides opportunities. That's how it happened for me. An advertisement I accidentally saw, some recommended books and authors, and conversations on the topic were my first timid and uncertain steps toward taking my health into my own hands. At first, I felt fear and scepticism about the new information and tested it with suspicion. Well, the results were not always encouraging, but at some point, I started feeling the difference, and the people around me were noticing it, too. Seeing how little by little my condition was improving, I gained more confidence and faith that I was on the right path. Today, five years later, I once again fully embrace life and the opportunities it offers. Much of what I have learned is an integral part of my daily routine, and I resort to other means only in certain cases. I feel stronger, and I know that everyone's mental and physical well-being is in their own hands and requires constant care. Life goes on with all its variety, the ups and downs being an essential part of it. That's why it's good to be able to rely on ourselves and some practices that can help us go through difficult periods more easily.

Each page of this book contains personal experience and techniques that I have tested myself. I want to emphasize that I did not invent these practices; they are existing techniques that I have tried out and found really helpful. At the same time, I am fully aware that not everything that has worked for me will work for you since every person is unique.

Dear reader, I do hope that while reading my book, you will discover a lot of things to borrow and incorporate into your life.

The perspective on all means and techniques covered in the book and their application will help you regain control over your life and shake off your fears, sadness and anxiety. And when that happens, I'll be thrilled, knowing that I have been of at least some help to you.

So, let's begin! Arm yourself with courage, patience, and curiosity, and then we can take the first step together!

STRUCTURE OF THE BOOK

The book is divided into chapters, each focusing on a different technique or a basic health-supporting practice. All chapters contain useful information and applying the learned will surely improve your health. To me, the most important of all is the chapter dedicated to food, since I believe that what we put on our plates largely determines how we feel.

The book is structured in such a way that it can be read sequentially or by selecting certain parts that currently interest you the most. Each section contains additional space for personal notes, and the last part of the book provides an opportunity to choose the most important personal practices for you and outline the steps to improving your health. However you approach the book, don't be afraid to skip some practices and give your preference to others. This is your journey, and you know best how to travel it.

Whatever your choice, I would advise you to read the book not as fiction, but to give yourself the necessary time to make sense of the written and introduce it into your life. It is good to take notes and use the special spaces in the book to write down the parts that are most important to you. If you prefer, you can have a separate personal diary for your notes, and, I think, it's a good idea to use it every day. You can also feel free to highlight or mark certain parts of the text that you find important. After all, the purpose is to get the most out of the book, in the way that works best for you, not to keep it intact.

PILLARS OF HEALTH

I believe that our health rests on several pillars: what we eat, what we drink, the quality of our sleep, how we rest, how we have fun, what thoughts occupy our minds and what faith we have. In fact, our well-being depends to a great extent on their quality. If your pillars are different or you want to add some more, don't hesitate to include them.

Now, let's dive into each of these pillars.

FOOD

I'd like to start with the well-known Hippocrates quote: "Let food be thy medicine and medicine be thy food!". This saying is particularly relevant today when the critical approach to what we put on our plate should be our top priority.

Hardly ever in the history of humanity have Western societies had such a variety of food, and yet it is hard to believe that society as a whole has ever been so poorly nourished. Food temptations lurk around every single corner. Television commercials persuade us to try a new sandwich or fries at a fast-food restaurant. Food chains offer us an abundance of a la minutes, heat-only pizzas or soup that we cook in minutes by simply adding boiling water. Everything seems delicious and, sometimes, even healthy until we look at the ingredients label and see chemicals or dubious elements whose names rarely tell us anything. In our desire for instant ready meals, we delegate the decision of what to put on our table to TV commercials.

It's well-known that ads are an extremely strong trigger for food choices and that fooled by TV we often choose food that satisfies us physically and emotionally but doesn't provide our bodies with the necessary vitamins, minerals, and essential nutrients. It seems like we push aside the consequences and what we are causing ourselves. Even when encountering a health problem, we rarely seek the link between what we eat and our health. We refuse to see that in recent years things have changed significantly and we cannot solely blame contemporary stress for all our problems while claiming that our grandparents used to eat almost the same food.

In light of this, few people have decided to prioritize healthy eating, but even then, there are many myths that can steer us wrong. We live in a world of information plenty which often complicates our choices instead of making them easier. Celebrities preach specific feeding regimes and label them healthy amid ever-changing diets and food trends like vegetarian, vegan, paleo, keto, and what-not which are some of the diets people choose to solve certain problems. However, the benefits of a regime are often only temporary, sometimes lacking at all, or even worse, it can harm us. Media also does not help, instead, they are flooding us with contradictory and sometimes even unsafe information. Foods that one day have the status of healthy or superfoods, the next day are replaced by a new diet trend.

Dealing with such a situation and finding a dietary regime that aligns with your preferences and, at the same time, supports your health is extremely challenging. There are hundreds of people who, after stepping on the path of healthy eating, still struggle to find the answers to many questions like: Should I eat fruit, or their sugar content is so high that it's better to avoid them? Should I consume juices, smoothies, or fresh juices? How do I balance the fat and protein content in my daily menu to maintain my health? Do I need fats, and if so, which ones exactly? And what about carbohydrates? Should I exclude them from my diet? What does my body need, and what are my brain's needs? The answers to these questions are not straightforward and often depend on the sources we refer to and trust. Besides the information we get is frequently contradictory. Even when we have clarity on these questions and the path we want to follow, things do not get any easier. Restaurants and eateries often offer food that is heavily oriented toward modern eating trends, so finding alternative options can be quite a challenge. For example, a lot of people do not consume gluten, yet gluten-free alternatives are still not widely available, and even when they are, they often rely heavily on corn. Menus rarely list all allergenic foods, and vegan eateries predominantly offer vegan meat alternatives and a scarce choice of salads and plant-based foods. Thus, the desire for healthy eating outside the home often proves to be difficult to achieve. In addition, anyone daring to deviate from the accepted dietary standards, i.e., the food offered in eating houses (high-fat, fried foods), risks being misunderstood by their circle of friends and labelled as an outsider or a freak, which is a social factor that we can hardly ignore.

On the other hand, while at home and chasing time we often face the need to buy something quickly from the neighbourhood store where temptations with harmful additives sneak right up on us from every shelf. Foods often contain preservatives, stabilizers, flavours and flavour enhancers which surely won't restore your health, and what's worse, may even cause health problems one day. Reading the labels of every food item can certainly become a tedious and stressful activity, and as a result, we may simply stop scrutinizing and start repeating to ourselves that it probably won't make much of a difference and that so many people consume these things without any issues. This is a statement far from the truth because our health depends on every single choice we make and sooner or later we will face the accumulated result of our bad choices.

For me, finding the right nutritional approach was a long process of trial and error. Without a doubt though, the nutritional guidance of the Medical Medium Anthony William[1] proved to be my turning point. It answered all my questions and gave me a deeper understanding of the human body and the direct link between food and health. Moreover, it became the springboard for my improvement and my current regimen is fully built on it. The information that he presents is of great importance to contemporary people and of vital importance to those suffering from chronic diseases and complaints, offering a path to cure. This is the reason I highly recommend his books, as well as his health-related shows which will help and give direction while coping with health problems, spotlighting the dangers we face today and ways to combat them. So, I'd like to emphasize again that his books would be extremely helpful especially if you have any health issues.

When it comes to what to eat, be sure to include plenty of vegetables and fruits in your meals. Take on clean eating and avoid preservatives, stabilizers, and artificial flavours. Spice up your food naturally with parsley, coriander, oregano, rosemary, thyme, and sage. To retain the maximum nutrition in products, avoid overcooking. Reduce fat intake (add little coconut or avocado oil when cooking or no fat at all) and use less salt. Remember that leafy green salads are the better choice and fruits should take a special place in your routine. Add freshly made fruit and vegetable juices and smoothies that are not only absolutely delicious but also quickly supply your body with vitamins and minerals. If due to a health issue, you can't drink juices or have concerns with that, try to eat more fruit instead. Don't be afraid of fruits and the sugar in them as it is a different kind of sugar that is needed by your body. In addition, add to your daily meals potatoes especially when boiled or baked.

---

[1] www.medicalmedium.com

4

Build a relationship with food. Chew it longer and be present while eating. Eat with your eyes and don't let negative thoughts affect you. Stop eating your anger or in other words, don't eat until you've calmed down.

Prepare your food so you are delighted with the way it looks. We often eat with our eyes so it is important to like the food we see. Using a wide range of spices and fresh ingredients will help you in creating a different nutritional approach.

In case you struggle with your weight don't be too focused on its loss. Often, people rush to lose weight starving themselves, without realizing that their body needs food and the goal above all should be health, not appearance. Eating healthy and quality food can never do harm. Remember your brain needs carbs, so don't deprive it of sweet foods, but stay away from white sugar, sweeteners, glucose-fructose syrup and other harmful ingredients. Prefer healthy alternatives like honey, or fruits like bananas and mangoes that can be eaten anytime, as well as their dried version including my favourite dates, apricots, and figs. Besides satisfying our sweet tooth, they are also a reliable source of vitamins and minerals.

When talking about food, we cannot help but mention the topic of forbidden food. Are there things we need to abstain from while healing or we are allowed to indulge in everything? As I mentioned earlier, my diet is completely based on the recommendations of the Medical Medium Anthony William, who excludes the consumption of gluten, dairy products, eggs, and vinegar. I am fully aware that the current information regarding gluten is quite controversial and that it is very difficult to give up something so embedded in our daily diet, and that it is not easy to give up foods we grew up with. However, I am convinced that when a person is dealing with a health problem, removing these foods from their menu is crucial and the improvement it leads to is definitely worth it. Thus, if you struggle with a condition, I advise you to give it a try by gradually eliminating the foods listed by the Medical Medium Anthony William as non-foods. You may start with 1 or 2 of them to see how you feel and then drop the rest one by one.

Whatever decision you make and whatever path you choose remember that every person is unique and that you have to learn to listen to your body's signals. Real change takes time. Choose the food you put in your body guided by self-love and you can be sure that your efforts shall be rewarded sooner or later. Opt for fruits and vegetables, clean and fresh food and you'll feel the difference very soon.

Make changes slowly and give yourself plenty of time. Too many changes in a short period of time will cause unnecessary stress and, instead of helping, might even worsen things. Listen to your body and if you feel something is too much for you, take a step back and slow down.

The important thing is to feel joy in what you are doing. Keep in mind that it's all for your own good and the results won't be long in coming.

<u>Your notes</u>:

<u>1-3 things to use in the future</u>:

WATER

Water! So valuable and vital for humans! A person can survive a few days without water. Considering the amount of water in the human body, which varies between 45-75%, it is not surprising how essential it is for our existence. I'd like to note that both the quality and the quantity we consume daily are of great importance. Nowadays, a large part of the Western society has free access to drinking water; unfortunately, it's not always as good as it should be.

On the one hand, this is due to the water pipes (outdated in many places), and on the other hand, water often contains pollutants such as chemical elements, toxins, pathogens and others, that are harmful to us. Disinfectants like fluoride and chlorine that are added to clear it from pathogens are definitely not healthy.

Fortunately, this problem can be easily resolved as the market nowadays offers a variety of water purification systems: reverse osmosis, filter jugs and others, even more advanced. With so many options available, choosing the right system for water purification can be a challenging task, and in some cases, a serious financial investment. However, remember that the goal of drinking water free of chemicals or harmful substances is worth all the effort and investment.

Therefore, my advice to you is to approach this issue seriously and conduct your own research. Note down your main requirements and conduct an investigation before choosing a water purification machine or filter. I myself use a water filtering system, ensuring clean water on my table at all times. When choosing it, I was guided mainly by the capacity and quality of the filter, i.e., what chemicals and particles it can sieve and in what percentages.

When buying water from the store, I would advise you to opt for those in glass bottles. Choose pure spring water and don't be deceived by trendy waters with added flavours, vitamins and minerals, which often conceal other not-so-beneficial ingredients. Even if you choose plastic bottles, there is no need to worry, just try to avoid their everyday use.

Speaking of the secrets and wonders of water, it is worth mentioning the Japanese businessman Masaru Emoto and his research work on the structure of water. He discovered that water responds to our words by changing its structure and forming beautiful crystal shapes. It is interesting to see the shapes after words of love and compassion and then compare them to those formed after words of hatred and fear. The discovery of Masaru Emoto can be applied in our daily lives by either speaking to water or placing labels with messages of love and happiness on water containers. This is supposed to make the structure of the water positive so that it would exert a beneficial effect on our bodies. You may try different messages such as "health," "happiness," "light," etc.

Besides the quality of water, it is necessary to pay attention to the quantity you consume daily. Generally, daily intake is strictly individual and closely related to the other fluids we drink and the food we eat. For example, tea and coffee are diuretics, and you should not calculate them in your daily water intake. On the other hand, consuming more raw fruit, vegetables and juices, will certainly reduce your need for additional water due to their high water content. Try to drink as much water as you can (for example 2 litres), distributed throughout the day. In accordance with the recommendations of the Medical Medium Anthony William, I start my day with 1 litre of room temperature water mixed with the juice of one lemon which aids in cleansing the liver. Of course, you can start with a smaller amount like 500 ml of water and the juice of half a lemon or even less, if you prefer so.

I usually drink my daily water regularly and consistently throughout the day adding lemon juice whenever possible. If 2 litres of water seem like too much or if you find it difficult to drink plain water, you can try to enhance its taste by adding herbs or fruits/vegetables, such as mint, thyme, sliced ginger, lemon slices, orange, cucumber, etc. The options are endless and, besides adding flavour, they will also enrich it with nutrients. I guarantee you will soon feel the difference just by drinking more water.

In certain cases, it is absolutely necessary to increase even more your water intake. For example, if you have a headache, slept poorly or not enough, or feel unwell, proper hydration can be of great help. The next time you are out of sorts, give it a try, and you will see how with each glass of water you'll be feeling better and better. This is a strategy I have tested myself and I can only assure you how good it works.

Personally, whenever I haven't slept well or feel indisposed, I consciously increase the amount of water I drink, and even after the first litre, I feel much better.

In fact, on days when I've been on the move or, for some other reason, have had less water, my body immediately reacts, often with a headache.

In case you're wondering whether you drink enough water, perhaps the easiest way to find out is by checking the colour of your urine. For example, dark-coloured urine indicates dehydration and should remind you to increase your water intake. When properly hydrated, urine has a light colour. Another indication of adequate water intake is frequent visits to the toilet. I know it is annoying, but don't get discouraged. Your overall health worths it.

Perhaps, the most challenging part is to turn the regular drinking of water into a habit. In our fast-paced daily lives, we often forget about it and, in many cases, the signals of thirst are mistaken for hunger. In this regard, it's helpful to have a system that gives you an idea of the amount of water you have consumed and reminds to reach for it. An effective way is to pour water into a bottle and keep track of the quantities you drink. You can also use a glass of a certain measurement. A good hack for developing a habit is to set an alarm or use another method of reminding yourself to take sips of water. The best tactic is to drink water regularly, without waiting to feel thirsty because by this time you may already be dehydrated. It's a good idea to drink the largest portion after getting up and take the rest regularly and consistently throughout the day.

Often, talking about daily water intake, people mean all the beverages they have consumed, not realizing that not all of them have the same hydrating properties as water. And since we are surrounded by a great variety of drinks to choose from such as coffee, tea, soft drinks, alcoholic and energy drinks, etc., water often takes a back seat and unfairly receives less attention than it deserves.

Let's not forget there are beverages that not only fail to hydrate us but also have no beneficial health effects. I would definitely advise you to stop consuming carbonated soft drinks, which often contain harmful ingredients and a large amount of sugar, and to cut down on caffeine. If you find it difficult to completely give them up, try to decrease their consumption or replace them with something healthier like 100% natural fruit juices. Giving up caffeine may seem like an impossible mission for many people, especially when it has become a ritual to start the day with a cup of coffee and have another one or even more later when we feel drowsy or tired. Yes, caffeine boosts adrenaline but it also has a particularly negative effect on people suffering from anxiety, restlessness, mood disorders, panic attacks, etc. Therefore, excluding caffeine from their daily menu is of utmost importance. It's worth noting that caffeine is present in many beverages, including black and green tea, cola, coffee, energy drinks, etc. If you have made up your mind to give it up, do it slowly, taking small steps and gradually reducing its consumption.

Another step forward is to try to cut down on alcohol as much as you can, or even give it up altogether. Again, like caffeine, alcohol has a negative impact on health, especially for people suffering from anxiety and emotional problems.

For me, giving up alcohol was one of the major steps I took, mainly because of its social aspect and the common belief that you need a drink when you have fun with friends, celebrate special occasions or just want to relax after a hard day. The truth is that when you are not feeling well, or you have a health issue, you should pay more attention to the things that exacerbate your symptoms and try to avoid them. If you decide to give up alcohol, start slowly by gradually limiting the occasions when you have a drink and reducing the quantities; over time, reserve its consumption for truly special moments. Remember that it's normal to experience difficulties and don't give up. As with everything mentioned so far, listen to your inner voice and take small but consistent steps forward.

After going through the list of beverages it's good to eliminate from your diet, I will conclude this chapter with the magical drink that, in my opinion, you should incorporate into your daily routine if you want to help your body and mind feel better. That's the healing celery juice. For years, the Medical Medium Anthony William, who is the founder of the global celery juice movement, has been talking about the benefits of drinking celery juice. It helps against viruses, bacteria, toxic acids, fungi, pesticides, herbicides, heavy metals, petrochemicals, and many others. No wonder thousands of people around the world, including some celebrities, have turned the morning drinking of celery juice into a ritual. You can find more information about its healing properties on the Internet[2].

Celery juice is best consumed pure, without mixing it with other vegetables or fruits or diluting it with water. You should also avoid eating or drinking 15-30 minutes before and after it. The optimal

---

[2] https://www.medicalmedium.com/medical-medium-blog-celery-juice.htm

quantity of celery juice is 500 ml to a maximum of 1 litre per day. You'd better start with small amounts and gradually increase them. For how to prepare and drink it and the full list of its benefits, I recommend the book "Celery Juice" by Anthony William, who popularized its consumption all over the world.

For me, drinking celery juice was definitely no love at first sight. I found the taste and smell very strong and it took me quite a long time to get used to it. It was a year or two before I got used to the taste and I sometimes even enjoyed it. Due to its powerful healing effect, I had stomach pangs for a while after drinking it, but the wonderful effect I noticed on my skin, body and mind within a few months was definitely worth the effort. Nowadays, I drink around 1 litre of celery juice every day and I feel perfect.

Your notes:

1-3 things to use in the future:

SLEEP

The role of sleep in our well-being is extremely important. We need sleep not only on a physical level, for the regeneration and recovery of our bodies, but also on an emotional and mental level for processing the emotions accumulated throughout the day. There is even a saying that goes: "Sleep on a decision or a problem".

Our body also recognizes the role of sleep, and that's why when we feel unwell or fight a virus or physical discomfort, we tend to sleep more in line with the other saying "Sleep heals."

Contrary to all said above about sleep, it seems that nowadays, people consciously sleep less, influenced by the dynamics and intensity of present-day life. Free time that should be spent to catch up on some sleep is often wasted on watching movies, television, surfing the Internet, late-night socializing, or doing something urgent. We like saying that no one makes memories while sleeping and strive to live life to the fullest, being aware that we limit the time our bodies need to rest and recharge. Sleep is crucial for feeling refreshed, well-rested, and better equipped to face life's challenges and, what's more, it supports the normal functioning of our nervous system. In this context, it is quite worrying that the average duration of sleep has decreased compared to previous generations when the lack of electricity, television and other forms of entertainment meant going to bed earlier and getting more sleep.

The average person needs between 7-8 hours of sleep per night to function properly, and for many, even these are insufficient. This indicator is highly individual and largely dependent on lifestyle, the intensity of daily activities and each person's overall health condition. The question is not only to find out how much sleep do we need but also to provide ourselves with it. The majority of people live in the cycle of chronic sleep deprivation, eagerly awaiting the long-dreamed holiday or the weekend to catch up on sleep while continuing to go to bed late and get up early day after day.

However, not only the quantity of sleep but also its quality matters, i.e., how well we sleep, how many times we wake up, and whether it is difficult for us to fall asleep. We can easily assess how restorative our night was based on how we felt upon waking up the next morning and throughout the whole day. In recent years, the number of people experiencing sleep issues, such as difficulty falling asleep, frequent awakenings, or inability to fall back asleep, has been increasing. After such nights, people feel tired, moody and drowsy. The problem intensifies when sleep issues become more frequent, and as a result, the mere thought of going to bed fills us with anxiety about the coming night. Taking into account the seriousness of the problem and the number of affected people, it is not surprising that the number of TV commercials offering solutions continues to grow. Whether and to what extent they help is a question that each person can answer for themselves; and if they do help, is this really the health alternative our body deserves?

I didn't realize the importance of this pillar for a long time, and for that reason, I paid little attention to it. While raising my son, who until the age of 4 would wake up several times during the night, I had intercepted sleep which over time, became so disrupted that it was extremely difficult for me to fall back asleep. And when I finally did, after hours of tossing and turning in bed, I would have a light and fragmented sleep, waking up from the slightest noise. As you can imagine, after such nights, I definitely didn't feel well throughout the day, and my time seemed to pass in a kind of foggy state. It's not surprising that headaches and fatigue became my frequent companions. Anyone who has had sleep problems is familiar with the deep effect they have on our overall well-being and normal functioning. Considering this, I can say that sleep improvement played a vital role in my recovery journey. It took me ages to learn to fall asleep more easily, to sleep deeply and not to wake up from every single noise. To achieve this, I had to make some changes in my daily routine and work on my overall health.

Having gone through sleep disorders, I am now fully aware of the importance of good sleep to my overall condition. Therefore, I take a serious and careful approach to the quality and quantity of sleep which are my priorities. If you suffer from insomnia or simply want to improve your sleep quality, you may find the following sleep hygiene tips useful:

- Try to go to bed and get up at the same time. On rest days, try to stick to your evening routine but allow yourself the sleep your body needs and indulge in the luxury of sleeping more.
- Try to go to bed earlier, preferably in the 9:00–10:00 pm range. Going to bed early has a more restorative and healing effect. It is well-known that every hour of sleep before midnight is worth two after midnight. Dr. Matt Walker, head of the Sleep and Neuroimaging Lab at the University of California, Berkeley, says your sleep quality does change as the night wears on.
- Make sure the room temperature is neither too cold nor too hot. Generally, it is recommended to sleep in a cooler room, which I myself prefer. So, in winter I avoid turning on the heating in the room where I sleep which provides fresh and slightly cool air. Some people prefer to sleep in warmer conditions but I think it's mostly a matter of habit that can be easily overcome by gradually lowering the temperature. When you get used to sleeping at lower temperatures, you will notice that it helps you feel fresher and more rested the next day.
- Ventilate the room and make sure it is sufficiently dark. For this purpose, use thick curtains or blackout blinds. Darkness will help you sleep better since our bodies produce the sleep hormone melatonin in the absence of light during the night.

If you don't have blinds or curtains, you can use an eye mask to protect your eyes from light.

- Silence is also important for good sleep. If you are sensitive to noise, this can be a problem, especially if you live in a noisy part of the city. In such cases, you may use earplugs or noise-cancelling headphones. Phone applications with the so-called white noise also help for falling asleep. You can choose the white noise that relaxes you the most, such as the sound of the ocean, running water and so on.

- Wear comfortable, lightweight and loose sleepwear. Whenever possible, choose clothes, bed sheets and blankets made of natural materials like 100% cotton and avoid synthetic fabrics.

- Turn your room into a cozy and comfortable place and avoid air fresheners and strong scents. Besides being harmful to your health, they will not allow your nervous system to relax and recover.

- Develop a habit of not watching television, working on the computer or using your phone one hour before bedtime. The blue light of the screens is not only harmful to the eyes but also stimulates the brain and worsens the quality of sleep. If you find this difficult, you can use special glasses that neutralize the effects of blue light. Besides the blue light, the content of what you watch can further frighten you or stimulate your nervous system.

- One hour before bedtime, try to relax and tune into a sleep wave. Leave work problems for the next day and do something pleasant. Avoid news, negative thoughts and serious conversations during this time.

- Create your own evening ritual, which facilitates a smoother transition to sleep, such as taking a warm shower, reading a book, engaging in light conversations with loved ones, etc.

- It is helpful to shut off all thoughts about work and unfinished tasks by telling yourself they belong to the past day and that tomorrow will provide you with strength and enough time to handle every surprise life is to offer. This may be one of the most challenging tasks but keep reminding yourself that the day is for focusing on work, while the evening is time for recovery. You can mentally repeat as a mantra that you will deal with the thoughts that upset you tomorrow and that now you are relaxing and preparing for sleep.

- Avoid exercising before bedtime. Light physical exercises, stretching, and meditation in the early evening hours can be beneficial but you can miss them if you want. When you feel tense and nervous, remember that yoga offers special exercises for relaxing and promoting good sleep. You can try lying on the floor, raising your legs and holding the outer edges of your feet, or lifting your legs up against the wall. The child's pose with your arms alongside your thighs and the palms facing upwards is another alternative.

- Try yoga nidra, which helps both fast falling asleep and relaxation. The Internet offers various yoga nidra practices of different durations that you can do at home. They will help you understand this form of yoga and feel its effects.

- Avoid caffeine and stimulating drinks in the second half of the day, including coffee, black and green tea, energy drinks, and even everyone's favourite, chocolate. If you cannot avoid them, try to reduce their consumption.

- In the evening, use soothing herbal teas, such as lemon balm, chamomile or lavender.

- You can indulge yourself in having a relaxing bath if you can afford it.

- Certain scents such as lavender have calming and relaxing properties. You can use it dried or its essential oil. I prefer the small sachets with dried lavender, which you can buy or make yourself, and place them in your wardrobe or under your pillow. The lavender scent will relax and calm you throughout the night.

- During the day, engage in physical activity – exercise, yoga, sports, etc. – or just try to spend some time outdoors. Physical movement and fresh air will recharge you and improve your sleep.

- Prefer inspiring or calming conversations in the hour before bedtime.
- Engage in journal writing and reflection on the good things in life.
- Listen to light and relaxing music.
- Identify the root cause of your poor sleep and take action to reduce its effect. Sometimes it can be something very trivial such as going to bed later than the usual time, which once corrected, may totally change things.
- Expand the list with other practices that you have found working for you.

As extensive as this list may seem, it is certainly not exhaustive, and you can always add other practices that have helped you or your loved ones. Start implementing them by trying out the tips one by one. It's important to arm yourself with patience and have faith that things will improve, no matter how long it may take. For milder sleep issues homeopathy, as well as many natural remedies, such as lavender or passionflower, can also be helpful. If you choose this path, it's good to find an experienced classical homeopath or naturopath who can give you advice about how to address insomnia.

However, if you suffer from acute insomnia or other disorders, it's advisable to consult a doctor.

Your notes:

1-3 things to use in the future:

REST AND RECREATION

Taking proper rest and self-care is another important pillar of our well-being. While sleep plays a significant role in our daily recovery, it alone is not sufficient to fully recharge us after long periods of challenges. A few days off now and then is of immense importance for overcoming stress, problems and difficulties. Just like with sleep, the need for a longer rest is strictly individual and depends on both our overall physical condition and the level and duration of stress.

Though we have the weekends, we should not overlook the role of holidays. Some people prefer taking a few days off more frequently throughout the year to recharge and recover. Others need longer vacations during the year to completely break away from daily responsibilities and commitments. The feasibility of this greatly depends on the nature of one's work and personal preferences.

A common feature of human nature is to ignore our needs until they become urgent, but at this point, it is either too late or we have reached a state that requires much more time to replenish our reserves. Conversely, when self-care is a priority and we dedicate time to rest and relaxation regularly, even in the face of daily demands, there will be no moments of exhaustion and we'll recover faster. In this sense, the best thing to do is to incorporate a little rest into our daily routine. This can be achieved by paying attention to how our daily life unfolds. If our job is predominantly physical, it is good to make time for something we enjoy that involves light or no physical exertion like reading a book, watching a favourite movie, engaging in a creative activity, listening to music, socializing with friends and loved ones, etc. On the other hand, if our work lacks physical activity, and we sit at a desk all day, it is good to engage in movement or exercise before or after the workday and consider options such as walking, cycling, using stairs more often, taking short walks during lunch breaks and so on.

Apart from physical movement, it is necessary to take care of our brain by taking short breaks at regular intervals, depending on the nature of our work. These breaks can be used for stretching, diverting focus briefly away from work, drinking a glass of water, or eating fresh or dried fruit. They have a calming and energizing effect, while also restoring and boosting our productivity. To experience the benefits of these pauses, try to include more of them into your routine over a period of a few days.

Regardless of the chores that await you in the evening at home, try to steal a few minutes for yourself to do something you genuinely enjoy and that makes you feel good. For example, I love drawing, reading books, watching something funny or relaxing on TV, listening to podcasts or personal development courses. The time I set aside for myself always feels short and flies away fast, but it's me time when I indulge in activities that truly recharge me. Often, this is the time when everyone is in bed, and when in the quiet of the night, I can dedicate it solely to myself and experience the magic of self-care.

Use Saturdays and Sundays for a complete break from the workweek. Make time for an activity that truly makes you feel relaxed. Plan outings with your family, meet up with friends, go to a restaurant, or simply be yourself. If you feel like resting, take a nap, slow down and allow things to happen at their own rhythm. Try to spend your weekends in a way that you enjoy the most, doing things that recharge you. Consider Saturdays and Sundays sacred days that have to be devoted to your well-being and use that time to give yourself the attention and care you deserve.

Try to bring more joy and fun into your life, and actively seek out the things that make you smile.

If you pay attention to your needs daily and give yourself the necessary rest, you will rarely feel exhausted and anxiously awaiting the annual vacation as it happens with many people. Remember that during periods of stress and increased workload, one needs more rest, and you don't have to wait until the planned annual vacation which may be several months away. During such periods, giving yourself proper care should become your number one priority.

Always listen to your body and pay attention to its signals; focus on the things that help you recreate yourself and feel happy.

When you realize and appreciate the importance of daily rest and recovery, and start taking care of yourself, you will notice how you become more stable and better prepared for stressful and tiring situations.

Your notes:

1-3 things to use in the future:

THOUGHTS

To emphasize the extraordinary importance of our thoughts, I'd like to begin this chapter with a quote from Buddha: "What you think, you become". According to studies, the average person has about 12,000-60,000 thoughts per day 80% of which are negative and 95% repetitive[3]. These numbers are certainly alarming. We can hardly imagine how much of our daily lives we spend on negative thoughts that affect our emotions and overall state, making us feel unhappy. With people suffering from anxiety, negative thoughts become even more intense, leading to the escalation of this condition and the emergence of other negative emotions.

Once those emotions arise, we are easily engulfed by them and start playing out negative scenarios, seeing problems even where there are none. If we surrender to those negative thoughts and emotions, we can be consumed by them, sinking deeper and deeper down the spiral. We often have no idea of what is happening and how these thoughts are gradually taking control over us and our lives. But if we understand how important our thoughts are and how they influence our feelings and emotions, we will be able to change them. Conscious striving to change our thoughts opens the path to positive emotions which trigger the domino effect and life begins to slowly change for the better. I guess, you understand that though it may sound easy, things in life do not happen that way since any change requires conscious effort, persistence and determination.

To realize the importance of thoughts and their effect on how we feel, you can conduct a simple experiment. Choose an unpleasant thought and focus on it briefly. For example, one of the thoughts I encounter with every new project at work is whether I will be able to handle it. If I choose to focus on the potential difficulties that this new task might bring, fear and the feeling of inadequacy will slowly

---

[3] Mind Matters: How To Effortlessly Have More Positive Thoughts | TLEX Institute

begin to arise. These may be coupled with some thoughts about whether I possess the necessary personal qualities, how realistic the deadlines are and whether I will be able to meet them. These are just a few of the doubts that would hover in my mind, besides I'd be totally unaware of the presence of a large part of them. If I give in to these thoughts, I would gradually get overwhelmed by anxiety and panic regarding my ability to cope with this new challenge.

Although illustrative, this example is very indicative of the way we often react mentally to challenges and difficulties. You can make an experiment by choosing a challenging situation and then trying to focus on its negative aspects. Allow the negative thoughts to occupy your mind for a few minutes, and then stop and try to assess your feelings and emotions. Most likely, you will find out that focusing on negative thoughts is a process where each negative thought leads to another, changing your mood and finally leaving you somewhat depressed. To feel the difference between negative and positive thoughts, it is good to conduct another experiment. Choose something pleasant and try to have only positive thoughts about it. Like in the previous experiment, you will see how your emotions change, this time leaving you happy or even unconsciously smiling. I guess, we all agree that positive thoughts make us feel better, more confident and open to life.

This is not my discovery. The power of thought has long been acknowledged and has become the foundation of many teachings. According to some of these, thoughts create our reality, so if we want to achieve a certain goal, it is good to think about it and behave in such a way as if the goal has already been achieved. I cannot say whether this is true or not, but I believe that the above experiments should convince us that directing our thoughts toward something positive makes us feel good. For that reason alone, it is worth keeping our thoughts under control and investing time and effort in their transformation. Here is a practice[4] that will definitely help you with that. First of all, try to find out how many and what kind of thoughts usually come to your head. However trivial it may sound, I assure you that you will be surprised by your thought pattern. In this phase, you will have to record every negative thought that comes to you for 2 weeks. I know it sounds easy but you will see that catching your thoughts is a challenging task. This is especially difficult if you have never paid attention to your thoughts before, so it's a good idea to have a small notebook with you at all times to write down every negative thought that arises in your mind. If you wonder how to distinguish negative thoughts from positive ones, whenever you have doubts, focus on how your thoughts make you feel. If what you are thinking at the moment makes you feel happy, fulfilled or smiling, you certainly don't need to write it down in your notebook. Conversely, if you feel scared, worried or sad, you should definitely write down that thought in your notebook. Considering that 80% of a person's average daily thoughts are negative, you can prepare yourself for a lot of entries, if of course, you approach this process with curiosity. Don't forget that negative thinking includes any self–criticism, such as "I won't succeed!", "I messed up so stupidly", "I can't handle it", "Everything bad always happens to me", "I'm so afraid to take this trip, to speak in front of those people, to take this step, etc.", as well as criticisms of others, blaming fate, other people, the day or whatever else for what has happened.

By recording and uncovering your thoughts, you will notice how often we criticize ourselves, approach situations negatively, and take on the position of being predestined to lose. Once you learn to pay attention to your thoughts and distinguish the negative ones, you can move on to the next step, which requires writing down the opposite positive thought for every identified negative thought. For example, the opposite of "I can't handle it" could be "I will try and see what happens. I might handle it." The opposite of "Everything bad always

---

[4] Lucinda Basset "From panic to power"

happens to me could be "Good things happen to me so often; failures are temporary and a normal part of life." The opposite of "I'm so afraid to take this trip, to speak in front of those people, to take this step, etc." could be "I'm so excited. It's completely normal to feel this way. This trip will bring me so many pleasant experiences. I have so many things to share with those people that will be helpful to them. I'm really thrilled about it."

Feel free to experiment boldly. There is no exact recipe for how a positive thought should sound, the important thing is that it makes you feel good. If it seems difficult to switch from a strongly negative thought to a positive one, start by experimenting with something more neutral like "I'll try, I have the desire, I feel ready to do it, etc."

With time, it will become easier and quicker for you to flip your thoughts into positive ones. The idea is to build new neurons in your brain that will change the way you think.

As a starting point, don't forget that it's extremely important to record both positive and negative thoughts. Trust me, no matter how much you want to skip this part or do it only mentally if you want the exercise to be successful, you need to do it in writing. Only then you can develop a true awareness of your thoughts and cultivate the habit of observing and transforming them. And with continuous practice and mindfulness, you will be able to more easily tune into a positive mindset and protect yourself from negative thoughts. When they arise, you should impartially acknowledge them by saying to yourself that they are just thoughts and thoughts alone do not define you. Don't be fooled into thinking that practicing this is easy, it's definitely worth doing though. This is a practice I constantly use, and when I notice negative thoughts, I tell myself that I am not my thoughts.

After replacing negative thoughts with positive ones, it's time to move on to the last step, which is to try to believe in the positive thoughts and not in the negative ones. A helpful approach in that direction is to consider negative thoughts as just thoughts and nothing more. Turn off your emotions or try to look on them as an external observer. Conversely, accept positive thoughts with the faith that they are true. Believe that good things are happening to you, that the bad isn't as bad as it may seem and it will all pass soon. Repeat to yourself that things are going well for you. You can go even further by attempting to visualize the positive thoughts and imagining how you would feel when they come true.

Remember that negative thoughts are a normal state, but you have the ability to change them and thereby change your life by introducing more positive thoughts, a more positive attitude towards life and more pleasant emotions.

Be gentle with yourself. Even when you're in a stressful situation and overwhelmed by many negative thoughts, it's good to remind yourself that they are just thoughts that won't last forever. Try to consciously redirect them towards something positive and believe that the positive things you imagine will happen. Approach everything with the mindset that our thoughts can create reality, which means that it's better to have good thoughts and trust they will come true, even if we don't believe them or have no idea of how this will happen.

When you start practicing, you may find everything very difficult and not changing fast enough. You will need a lot of patience and self-love for this process since it requires constant daily work; it's not something you learn once and never need to practice again. Keep trying, and sooner or later, you will be surprised by the results.

Other techniques you can try if you find yourself in a situation where your mind is overcrowded by many negative thoughts include solving puzzles, cooking, watching comedies, cleaning or engaging in any physical activity that requires concentration. Any activity that absorbs you and directs your thoughts towards something different will be beneficial. It's also good if you start learning something like knitting, drawing, working with ceramics, etc to engage your mind and create new thinking paths. Try different techniques and you'll see how helpful they are in pushing away most of your negative thoughts.

Your notes:

1-3 things to use in the future:

FAITH

In this chapter we will look at faith. There is no way I can leave it out of the scope of important practices because to me faith is the driving force behind every change, the fuel that keeps us going even in the most difficult moments. Talking about faith, I guess that many of you attribute religious significance to it and perhaps you are right. If you believe in the existence of God, Allah or any higher power, then most likely you believe that you are not alone in this world and this power protects and helps you, giving you strength and inspiration in times of difficulty and trial.

However, faith may be not only religious. Even if you are among those who do not believe in the existence of God or any power that is above us, you may still believe in science, yourself or something else.

While in moments when you feel good, faith may not be as necessary, in difficult situations or when struggling with a health issue it is extremely important to strengthen your faith – believe that regardless of the hardships you are facing, the situation will change, believe that your health can improve or that you can cope with the situation. With such faith, you will navigate through difficult moments and challenges more easily. In order to have faith on your side when needed, it is good to work on it daily.

Certainly, faith in any higher power can only be beneficial to you but if you don't resonate with that, then you can believe in the Universe, Life, some general force, energy, your body, your ability to cope, etc. Whatever it may be, do not let it die, but give it the necessary attention. If you give it the chance to develop and reinforce itself, this will make you stronger and more confident. When difficulties come, believe that they are temporary. Every time you make a step back, repeat to yourself that this will change and a time will come when you'll take more steps forward. Believe and you will be able to make better progress.

Your notes:

1-3 things to use in the future:

IMPORTANT PRACTICES

After discussing the fundamental pillars of health, it's time to focus on some practices that have helped me and thousands of people worldwide, which you can incorporate into your life. Just like with the previously discussed practices, it's important to experiment and try them out to assess how each resonates with you. Before giving up on any practice, my advice is that you give it enough time. Sometimes, things that are far from our understanding and past experiences may initially meet strong resistance, though, in the long run, they can bring many benefits to our health. Keep trying, listen to your body and give yourself the necessary time.

As with the other practices, I want to emphasize that none of the following was invented by me; I simply discovered them in my quest to feel better.

MEDITATION

In recent years it seems that meditation has largely entered the Western culture. And if only a few years ago it was rare to meet a person who openly admitted to meditating, nowadays almost everyone has heard of or tried meditation, and quite a few do it regularly. The practice of meditation by famous people and their open recognition of its benefits, the inclusion of meditation in yoga classes, as well as in a number of stress-reduction practices, also play a role in this. It is not by chance that large corporations are introducing meditation as part of their programs to improve their employees' health and mental state, some going so far as to provide special meditation rooms in the workplace.

The fame of meditation is directly linked to the benefits that regular meditation practices can bring. These benefits have been proven by numerous scientific studies, indicating that meditation helps in coping with stressful situations and anxiety, reducing negative emotions and experiences, improving sleep problems and stimulating positive emotions and experiences. Additionally, meditation helps us experience the present moment since its essence lies in returning to the present – here and now. It helps us better understand ourselves and be more tolerant and attentive to others. Through meditation, we develop the ability to be aware of how we feel in every moment, to sense where exactly the pain is and to be aware of the thoughts dominating our consciousness.

There are different definitions and approaches to meditation, depending on the teacher or the source. Each of them undoubtedly has its own benefits and their variety allows us to choose the one that best suits our individual preferences. To me, meditation is a state where, in silence, I focus on the present moment, observing my thoughts and the things happening in my world without emotionally attaching to them.

Meditation can be practiced in any posture – sitting, lying down, or walking. The most common method is sitting, usually on a chair or on the ground with crossed legs. If you're unsure whether to sit or lie down, it's important to consider that the sitting posture is more challenging since you should keep your back straight but not tense. Lying down meditations are not suitable if you easily fall asleep and prefer to really experience fully the meditation. In this case, it's better to opt for sitting meditations. However, if you feel more comfortable lying down, don't hesitate to choose that posture. No need to worry because even if you fall asleep, meditation still works on your subconscious mind and will do its job. Moving meditations are suitable for people who find it difficult to remain still and for those with dynamic daily lives.

Personally, I like to vary the types of meditation depending on my state. When I'm tired or my back feels strained, I choose lying meditation. On other occasions, I prefer to sit with my legs on the floor or crossed. Sometimes, I resort to meditation even when I feel exhausted. Falling asleep during it doesn't upset me at all because I know that I will magically wake up as soon as the meditation is over and I'll feel better. If I don't have the opportunity to meditate, I try to focus on my walking or simply close my eyes for a minute or two and listen to my breathing. It may sound strange but one of the most famous examples of a meditative state is dishwashing, where our attention is completely focused on what we are doing without allowing our thoughts to wander and hover over other topics.

If you want to meditate in a seated position but you feel discomfort while doing so – your back tenses up, or you can't stay upright for long – you can lean against the wall or something else. The important thing, in this case, is that your head should remain unpropped.

After you have chosen the type of meditation and adopted a suitable posture, spend some time in a state of stillness. In the beginning, it may be difficult – you may feel an itch or the need to fix your hair or move. While most meditation teachings advocate maintaining complete stillness during meditation, which should not be disturbed by any physical discomfort, there are teachers who advise addressing physical discomforts (such as a strong urge to scratch an itch or get a fly or mosquito off) in the lightest and possibly most focused way. If you can remain in a state of stillness, then do so, but if it creates more discomfort for you and your thoughts are constantly focused on that part of your body that wants to be scratched, then go ahead and address it. In most cases, maintaining absolute stillness while seated proves to be difficult for me. At first, any slight movement during meditation left me with a feeling of failure and a sense of not doing the meditation in the way I considered appropriate. It took me some time to learn to accept each meditation as it is, without burdening it with my personal expectations and evaluations. By changing my approach and realizing that each meditation best reflects the current moment, my enjoyment of practicing it increased.

Once we have assumed a comfortable posture, the next step is to decide whether to close our eyes or leave them open. Most meditations are done with closed eyes, but others can be done with our eyelids slightly lowered or even open. One such example is walking meditation, where the focus is on our steps rather than our breathing.

Regardless of the chosen meditation, you'd better leave any expectations aside and simply try to feel the present moment. Our thoughts will not stop and will continue to remind us of their presence even during the most ideal meditation, which is certainly not the goal. On the contrary, the approach should be that of observers who just register the appearance of thoughts without getting entangled in them. One technique that will assist us in this is to imagine our thoughts passing on a movie screen while we're only watching and registering them without emotions or attachment. Others suggest visualizing thoughts as clouds moving across the sky or as fish swimming in the water that we observe impartially. Whichever approach you choose, the main thing is to acknowledge the arising of thoughts without identifying with them, being aware they are just thoughts and that we are not our thoughts.

Many people are extremely critical of themselves, pursuing the ideal of a meditative practice where there are no stray thoughts, the focus is entirely on breathing and the goal is to reach a blissful state. This is far from reality, as our brains cannot remain idle. They constantly wander, seeking problems and subjects to contemplate. The practice of regular meditation helps us to increase those brief moments when we are focused on our breath. Nevertheless, each meditation is different and it is good to accept that while in some cases we may feel more present in the moment, in others, our thoughts will jump from one topic to another. At times, we may feel completely in sync with ourselves, while at other times, we may be stressed and tense. Regardless of our experience, the idea is to accept the situation and embrace it as it is, without burdening it with the disappointment of unfulfilled expectations and with no blaming or getting angry at ourselves.

The type of meditation and its duration can vary greatly. One of the most common meditations is where one's attention is focused on the breath, i.e., the cycles of inhalation and exhalation. Whenever we notice our thoughts wandering, we should try to redirect our attention back to the breathing – inhaling, exhaling. This cycle may repeat again and again because it is in our nature to keep thinking. To deal with the ceaseless stream of thoughts, some meditations use mantras – words that carry certain energetic and emotional charges which, when repeated, free our consciousness. Others require the meditators to repeat words such as "inhale" or "exhale" or even to count in their minds.

The goal of meditation determines the way it is practiced. If the goal is to be here and now, the focus is usually on the breath or observing our thoughts. The aim of other meditations is to help us cope with current problems, clear emotions, tune in and prepare for the fulfilment of a specific desire and so on. In these types of meditations, the focus is on visualizations – visualizing ourselves dealing with a health issue, envisioning our ideal day or life, coping with a current problem, feeling gratitude, etc. Guided meditations help in particular situations, for example, to relieve stress, prepare for the day, relax before sleep, etc. The possibilities are endless. If you want to try any of them, the easiest way is to search on the Internet (YouTube) or download one of the countless meditation apps on your phone which offer a rich selection, often free of charge.

You can experiment until you find meditations that make you feel good and affect you positively. Don't forget that in guided meditations the voice and style of the person leading the meditation are also important, so it is good to choose a practice that helps you relax without being a burden or causing additional stress.

The duration of meditation can also vary widely, depending on our individual needs and daily routines. Some last between 10-15 minutes, while others require more time – 45 minutes or even 1 hour.

However, regularity and consistency are crucial for your success. Doing a long meditation once a week is not the same as spending a few minutes every morning and evening. This is because in order to reprogram our brain neurons we have to make periodic efforts, i.e., practice regularly. Personally, I try to set aside time for meditation twice a day - morning and evening – for about 10-15 minutes. It doesn't always work out, and while some days I can spend more time and do more sessions, other times it may only be 5 minutes in the morning. Remember that every moment spent focusing on our breath and the present is worthwhile. In stressful and busy situations, this becomes even more important, as even 1-2 minutes of conscious breathing can be of help. Closing our eyes and tuning into the rhythm of our breath serve as "anchors" that firmly pull us back to the present moment.

In case of increased stress and a busy daily schedule, a good tip is not to be tempted to skip your practice. On the contrary, practice even more, despite everything. This will calm your nervous tension and enable you to face the challenges more mindfully.

Generally, it is desirable to perform meditations in a quiet and peaceful place where there is little risk of being suddenly interrupted. Choose a small spot in your home for doing the meditations. If you want or feel the need to create a relaxing and recharging atmosphere, you can use a favourite aromatic oil in a diffuser, light an unscented candle made of natural materials, listen to quiet meditation music or mantras, and so on. However, when this is not possible, and you are surrounded by noise instead of silence, you should not give up. Instead, apply the same tactic as with thoughts - observe the noise indifferently, without attachment.

One of my favourite meditations is the gradual body scan meditation, done in a lying position. This meditation has an incredible effect and helps us become aware of how we feel, sense if there is any pain or discomfort in any part of our bodies, and at the same time, get to know our bodies better. In this type of meditation, you need to lie down and gradually direct your attention to different body parts, starting, for example, with the toes of the right foot, then going on to the right sole, the area above the right knee, the right thigh, and then move to the left foot, the hips, the abdomen, the chest, the lower back, the right arm, the left arm, the shoulders, the neck and throat, the face, the ears and the head. If you feel any pain during this scan, it's good to stay in that area for a while, direct your attention to the pain and imagine that with each focused breath towards that pain it becomes smaller and smaller. If you want to try it out, follow this description or simply search for a body scan meditation on the Internet.

Let's conclude this chapter with a brief 5-minute practice focused on the breath. "Sit comfortably, with your back straight but not rigid. Close your eyes. Answer the question, ,Where am I?" Try to breathe slowly and deeply, tracking the path of each breath from the inhalation, then passing through the nose and down the chest; feel how it fills with air which gradually reaches your abdomen. Breathe out slowly as you feel the air passing again through the abdomen, the chest, the nose and leaving your body.

Focus on the inhalation and exhalation as you observe your abdomen expanding with each breath in and shrinking with each breath out.

If you feel that your attention is going away from your breath, acknowledge the thought just as an observer without getting emotionally attached to it, and then return to the breath.

Be here and now, with your attention focused on your breathing.

Try to extend the duration of the exhale. Inhale slowly, exhale more slowly. You can count up to 3 or 4 while inhaling, and up to 6 or 8 on exhaling.

Continue to inhale and exhale slowly. After a while, again slowly, bring your awareness back to your body. Recognize where you are and then slowly open your eyes.

Take a moment to notice how you feel.

Your notes:

1-3 things to use in the future:

RESPIRATORY PRACTICES

Respiratory practices?! Surely, for many of you, this sounds strange. Breathing is at the core of our existence – without air, we would last only a few minutes. It is an unconscious process regulated by the nervous system. However, the way we breathe can have a significant impact on the physiological and chemical processes taking place in our bodies.

The way we breathe and the quality of the air we inhale are both equally important for our health and well-being. In modern society, the air is often polluted, full of dust particles and harmful substances that affect our health. No wonder, in recent years, the sale of domestic air purifiers has increased. Thanks to their sophisticated filters, most of them remove not only dust particles but also viruses and bacteria, making them quite suitable for people with allergies and other respiratory issues.

Realizing the importance of the quality of the air we breathe, and the challenges posed by the fast-paced and industrial urban environment, some years ago, I decided to invest in an air purifier. It is a decision I have never regretted, especially during foggy days and nights, quite common in late autumn and winter. My machine provides clean air at all times, and anyone can feel the difference. Unfortunately, for those of us living in big cities, air pollution is increasingly noticeable due to the heavy traffic and the expanding industry. In some cities and countries, air pollution is one of the leading factors causing diseases and having a direct impact on life expectancy.

Recently, it has become extremely trendy to use various fragrances and air fresheners. I've been surprised to see how quickly these fragrances have taken over homes and public places and now are everywhere – in the perfumes of the people, in detergents and laundry softeners, in the air fresheners used in cars, taxis, public offices, shops and homes etc. Along with this trend, the number of people intolerant to such smells has also increased. Even if you are one of those who enjoy chemical scents in laundry detergents, car fresheners or those used in public stores and homes, you should consider how unhealthy these chemical fragrances really are. With all these smells surrounding us, it becomes almost impossible to perceive the real scent of life – that of flowers, trees and grass – which in my opinion, is the one that really makes us happy and calm.

Our health depends not only on the quality of the air we breathe but also on how we breathe. Unfortunately, it seems that modern people have forgotten how to breathe properly and how to use their breath in stressful situations. Breathing practices are respiratory exercises that, if performed regularly, can improve your health. Some of the benefits of these practices include stress reduction, increased lung capacity, etc. It is claimed that breathing practices help in combating stress and anxiety, improve sleep and immunity, and normalize blood pressure. Additionally, regular breathing exercises increase the elasticity and capacity of the lungs, which is particularly important during flu and cold seasons.

Breathing exercises are part of many ancient practices, where they have been used both therapeutically and for spiritual awakening and development. Some well-known practices are pranayama in yoga, breathing meditations in Buddhism, tai chi and others.

In the 1960s and 1970s, breathing practices underwent significant development, which continues to this day. New and different techniques and methods have emerged in the last 10-20 years. The differences are in the way the breathing is done – through the nose or mouth, whether we use the abdomen or diaphragm, the pace of breathing, periods of breath-holding (during inhalation or exhalation), the use of music, and so on.

All breathing practices should be performed on an empty stomach and in a way that does not cause excessive stress and tension. Perhaps, their strongest effect is felt in moments of stress and anxiety. Even a few deep conscious breaths or simply slowing down your breathing can be helpful in such moments. If you decide to engage in breathing practices, do them in short sessions – 2-3 minutes. Do not force yourself because this might make you feel dizzy. Regardless of the choice of breathing practices, always be guided by one primary goal - to feel better, calmer, and balanced. Do not rush into practices that require prolonged breath-holding and stress the body instead of helping it stabilize. Depending on your current state, some practices may not work well for you. Therefore, always listen to your body and its signals.

In case you decide to try a specific breathing practice, instead of just focusing on slow and deep breathing, there are many possibilities. I have included brief descriptions of diaphragmatic breathing, abdominal breathing, breath focus, square breathing, 4-7-8 breathing, alternate nostril breathing, lion's breath and the buzzing bee breath.

Abdominal breathing soothes the nervous system. To perform it, you need to relax while lying down or sitting. Inhalations are done through the nose, while you imagine the air gradually going down to the abdomen and then up again. With each inhalation the abdomen expands (you can easily feel it by placing your hand on it), then the air gradually moves up, filling the chest and reaching the collarbones. During exhalation, the air exits gradually, and the abdomen slowly sinks back down. Repeat this slowly a few times, and you will feel increasingly calm and relaxed.

Diaphragmatic breathing is similar to abdominal breathing, only here the focus is not on filling the abdomen with air but on expanding the diaphragm. The inhalation and exhalation should be primarily felt through the expansion and contraction of the diaphragm. Repeat several times.

Breath focus is mainly used in meditations where the mind is concentrated on the breath. The breathing is slow and conscious, inhaling and exhaling through the nose. You can repeat in your mind "inhale" with each inhalation and "exhale" with each exhalation.

In **square breathing**, inhalation and exhalation occur at equal intervals, accompanied by equal intervals of holding and waiting. You can start with an interval on 2 or 3 and gradually increase it. For example, if you choose an interval of 4, it means you count to 4 – inhalation, another 4 – hold, another 4 – exhalation, and again to 4 – hold. After a while, you can increase the interval to 5-6. It's all up to you but remember the goal is to enjoy it avoiding any stress or other negative effect. If done properly, this practice has an extremely calming and relaxing effect.

The 4-7-8 breathing technique is based on the principle of inhaling for 4 seconds (counts), holding for 7, and exhaling for 8. In this method, inhalation is done through the nose, counting to 4, then holding for 7, and exhalation is done through the mouth, counting to 8. To perform it, imagine you are following the sides of a triangle.

Bee-buzzing breath is particularly suitable for anxiety, anger, and confusion. It involves making a humming sound, hence its name. To do it, sit comfortably, close your eyes, and plug your ears with your hands. Inhale through the nose and while exhaling with a closed mouth (ears remain plugged), start humming for as long as you can. Repeat it three times.

Alternate nostril breathing helps with calming and relaxation. It is done in a seated position, preferably on the floor with crossed legs, both hands in mudras, namely: the right hand is with the index and middle fingers folded, and the left hand sits on the knees with the thumb and index finger touching. Start by closing the right nostril with the right thumb and inhaling through the left nostril. After inhalation, close the left nostril with the ring finger. Hold your breath. Open the right nostril and exhale. Slowly inhale through the right nostril. Close the nostril, hold, and exhale through the left nostril. When you decide to finish, exhale through the left nostril, get your hands off the nose, and resume normal breathing.

Lion's breath is performed from a seated position with hands placed on the knees and fingers spread apart. With eyes wide open, inhale through the nose, and when exhaling, open the mouth wide, stick out the tongue, and make a pronounced "ha" sound. Repeat the exercise 2-3 times.

These are just some of the numerous breathing practices. You can try each one of them to discover the ones that resonate deeply with you. Whatever your choice, don't forget that our breathing is here to help us keep self-control in every challenging, tense or stressful situation. So, when you feel like you're losing ground and facing another trial, simply stop and take a few deep and slow breaths, inhaling through the nose and exhaling through the nose or mouth. In general, slow and deep breathing helps increase blood oxygen levels and normalize our heart rate. When combined with the intention to be as present as possible in the current moment, you will gradually start to feel better and calmer.

Starting with a few breaths and gradually increasing the duration is indeed a good approach. Personally, I feel much better when I close my eyes and take a few deep breaths every time the pace of daily life is overwhelming or when I sense that I'm losing my footing. From my yoga practice, I really enjoy one variant of the alternate nostril breathing which I use for balancing and calming myself. It is done in the following way: breathe in and out through one nostril while keeping the other one shut, repeat it several times and then switch nostrils.

If after trying all the above methods you find that none of them works for you, you can still remember the power of slow and deep breathing can be of a help the next time you feel overwhelmed.

<u>Your notes</u>:

<u>1-3 things to use in the future</u>:

POSSITIVE AFFIRMATIONS

In the "Thoughts" chapter, we discussed their meaning and impact on our emotional and physical well-being.

Making daily efforts to replace negative thoughts with positive ones is particularly important considering that negative thoughts dominate our consciousness most of the time. To counteract them, we can use the so-called positive affirmations popularized by Louise Hay, the author of several self-help books, including the internationally renowned You Can Heal Your Life. Louise Hay introduced positive affirmations as an integral part of her life and even made use of them to treat various illnesses. Her books contain different affirmations suitable when addressing a number of health issues.

Some of her affirmations include: "It's only a thought, and a thought can be changed.", "As I say yes to life, life says yes to me.", "I am safe in the Universe and All Life loves and supports me,", "I release all negative thoughts of the past and all worries about the future.", "I release all drama from my life," and "I am loved, and I am at peace."

Here are a few of my favourites: "Everything in my world is in order," "Everything happens for my highest good," and "I am safe."

If you want to get familiar with more of her affirmations, you can read her books or simply search the internet.

You can also try to find other affirmations which will be extremely easy because the Internet, phone applications and books all offer a wealth from various authors, covering different areas of our lives. The role of affirmations is to energize us and make us feel good and confident and sometimes even a few short words can serve as a positive affirmation. In fact, there are no rules, and the only condition is to choose an affirmation that will help you shift the negative dialogue and make you feel better.

Another guideline in choosing an affirmation is to focus on what resonates with you the most. If you can't find one, you can easily create your own or modify an existing one. You will likely notice that depending on the situation, you use different affirmations. And that is completely normal because our environment determines our negative dialogue, against which we seek an antidote in the form of positive affirmations. For example, suitable affirmations for the workplace are those focused on our creativity, productivity, colleagues, nature of work, contributions to the organization, respect, recognition, professional and friendly relationships, etc. In times of uncertainty or problems, good affirmations are those that instil confidence that everything will work out and that things are unfolding in the best possible way. In our personal lives, we can use affirmations for harmony and love in our relationships, for building a wonderful family, for creating inspiring friendships, and for visiting new and beautiful places. We can work on every area of our lives by changing our focus and mindset to attract positive things.

Some affirmations can also be used in the form of questions[5] that direct our subconsciousness to perceive them as reality and seek ways to fulfil them. Examples include: "Why do I always feel so good and in inner peace and harmony?" or "Why do things always go so well for me?" or "Why am I highly valued at work?", etc.

The most challenging part about affirmations is holding your ground, especially when criticism or our negative voice is stronger. It is in our nature to criticize ourselves and we do it for everything—for situations that did not unfold as we expected, for our mistakes, and even for the actions and words of other people. And if, in a similar situation, we would approach a friend with understanding and words of comfort, to ourselves we rarely show sympathy but rather let our internal criticism swirl. Often, these negative dialogues have become an integral part of ourselves and we may even be unaware of their

---

[5] As per Vischen Lakhiani

existence. In most cases, they reflect the attitudes of others toward us. For example, if we were frequently criticized for something in our childhood, this may have left a deep trail in our minds, and in certain situations, we adopt and direct the same criticisms towards ourselves. Examples of such words might be, "I always mess things up!", "Nobody loves me!", "I can't do anything right!", "Everyone sees my flaws!", "Everything bad happens to me," "Nothing goes as it should," and many others of the sort.

Since these are thought patterns that have been built over the years, changing them requires a lot of time. Fortunately, if once we believed that the brain develops until a certain age after which changes are not possible, today we know that this is not true. We can learn new things, build new neural connections, and actually change existing thought patterns. And this is wonderful because, with persistence, we can learn to think more positively and with inspiration, i.e., to feel better and live better. This change happens through thought and action.

To incorporate affirmations into your life, start by choosing one or two that have a general significance in your life and resonate with you and your current state. Choose affirmations that are easy to remember, and if necessary, modify them according to your taste. You can draw inspiration from some of the following: "Everything in my world is in order!", "I feel wonderful!", "I enjoy excellent health!", "I am surrounded by wonderful people with whom I have harmonious relationships!", "Everything comes to me with ease!". When making your choice, go with the idea that they should represent a situation in your life the way you would like it to be and make you feel good. Try to believe in them when saying them. You may find it difficult at first, but over time, it will become easier for you to stop opposing or criticizing positive thoughts and start believing them. Be brave and experiment until you discover the affirmation(s) that resonate with you the most. Once you've made your choice, try to memorize them, for e.g., by writing them down and placing them in visible places (refrigerator, kitchen cabinet, bathroom, desk, etc.). The idea is to build the habit of repeating them consciously, thus consciously interrupting negative thoughts. To quickly build the habit of repeating positive words or phrases, you can use an alarm that will remind you to do it at certain intervals.

The idea is not only to get used to repeating affirmations but also, in situations when you face challenges, instead of seeing their negative side and giving up to fear, stress, or self-criticism, to be able to meet them with confidence, faith, and a positive mindset that everything is happening for your own good and in the best way possible.

To change your attitude towards certain areas of your life, you can use sets of ready-made affirmations in the form of cards, calendars, theme books, and others. I myself really like those in the form of cards. The best thing about them is that they cover a very wide range of areas and issues we can consciously bring light to with our positive thoughts. I usually choose two affirmations from different areas and place them on my desk while working. During breaks, my eyes often fall on them, and after reading them, I always feel a positive change. After a few days, I replace the affirmations with new ones, addressing another area.

This is definitely a practice worth trying! I know that you will enjoy it, and over time, you will see how these little words change your mindset toward life and make you look at everything in a more positive way.

Your notes:

1-3 things to use in the future:

MOVEMENT AND SPORT

I know we have all heard the popular sentence "Movement is health" or Aristotle's "Life requires movement" and, no doubt, we agree with them. However, the mode of life of modern humanity is the most sedentary ever in history.

While in the past, the majority of people were daily engaged in physical work and movement, nowadays most of us spend our days sitting at our workplaces, and even when the working day is over, instead of engaging ourselves in movement, we prefer to spend the evening on the couch in front of the television. We travel by cars and other means of transportation that facilitate our lives but limit our physical activity. It seems that new technologies, although meant to make our lives easier, work against us. Electric scooters, roller skates, and home exercise equipment not only fail to encourage us to move more but actually restrict our movement. At the same time, the convenience offered by cars, the habit and the speed of transportation are causing more and more people to choose driving over walking or biking. Many places previously accessible only by foot can now be reached by car further reducing the opportunities for movement. We are slowly getting used to the convenience of moving less, driving more, and resting, instead of walking, running, and simple movement.

Numerous studies give evidence of the benefits of movement and the harms of a sedentary lifestyle. It may sound strange but sitting is now regarded as the new smoking since lack of movement increases the risk of cardiovascular diseases, obesity, immobility, nervous system disorders, etc. It has been proven that regular physical activities have a positive effect on various aspects of our lives. They elevate our physical tone, boost our self-confidence and mood and maintain our muscles, bones and joints in good condition.

In recent years, there has been talk about the need for taking a certain number of steps every day in order to stay in good physical shape. The recommended number of steps varies according to different sources. While some recommend 10,000 steps per day, others consider their daily count to be between 5,000 and 7,000. No matter whether you count your steps or not, the important part is to be engaged in movement every day. One should consider their age and physical condition when determining the daily step count. Today people use modern bracelets or watches to measure their daily steps. Besides counting the steps, these devices often measure other indicators such as sleep quality and duration, heart activity and others. For those who don't feel like investing in special step-tracking devices, mobile phone applications can also help. Most phones have standard built-in applications but, if you want to try others, you can install a new one. Most of them offer information about the average weekly and monthly activity, which is useful in case we do not have the opportunity to move and fulfil our step goal every day due to weather conditions, commitments or our physical condition. However, it is important to compensate for low-activity days with higher-activity days so that our average monthly activity remains within the desired range. There are options for movement, even if our daily routine is more sedentary, like climbing the stairs to our floor instead of taking the elevator or walking to the nearby store instead of driving. Whenever possible, incorporate movement into your routine, such as taking a walk on a sunny day, walking to work, visiting a park on a day off, etc.

Walking is the most natural kind of movement. It has been established that making a single step engages around 200 muscles[6]. Just imagine how important it is for these muscles that we keep moving and, what's more, our energy and mood also get a boost.

Daily movement will definitely benefit you but it would be even better to include some sport in your daily lives. The kind of sport is a matter of personal preference and today we have a very wide choice.

---

[6] Which Muscles Are Used When You Walk? | UK Fitness Events Blog

For many, it can be fitness that helps build muscles or jogging that allows for tension release, toning and being in good shape. Others may choose sports clubs that offer group activities on a weekly basis or individual training. Those of us who prefer to organize our activities from the comfort of our own homes can turn to online yoga, Pilates, or dance classes, choosing the most convenient time for them. There are many options, and it all depends on our personal preferences and physical fitness. Don't forget that sports not only improve our physical condition but also enhance our self-confidence and mood. One of the reasons for this is the endorphin hormone released during exercise, making people feel good and acting as a natural painkiller. In addition, exercises reduce the levels of the stress hormones adrenaline and cortisol in our bodies.

Considering all these benefits, it's worth trying to be more physically active by incorporating periodic sports practice alongside daily movement. Start slowly and don't neglect your physical condition and abilities. If you don't feel fit, even a brief activity may have a positive effect, like for e.g., some light stretching. If your condition allows, engage in a favourite sport on a weekly basis.

Begin with a step count that suits your condition and try to slowly increase it over time. Another option is to strive for a certain number of daily steps and combine it with short stretching and muscle-tightening exercises. Utilize your rest days not only for relaxation but also for physical activities, such as walking in nature, cycling, etc., whenever the weather allows.

Always listen to your body. Don't compare yourself to others and don't follow any stereotypes about what and how much you should do each day. Do things step by step and you will soon find out that you can do more, and that you have become more confident and your body stronger, while at the same time, your mood and energy levels have increased.

Your notes:

1-3 things to use in the future:

NATURE

Nature is an important and inseparable part of our existence. Unfortunately, with the development of technology and the urbanization of society, it is becoming more distant and often missing in our lives. Big cities captivate us with their dynamics and entertainment. Life spins us around and even the thought of a brief and rejuvenating encounter with nature often fades. The opportunities to connect with it and breathe clean fresh air become increasingly limited and much dependent on where we live.

Regardless of our busy routines and lack of time, the connection with nature should be a priority for anyone with a health problem or wanting to prevent one. Besides clean air, encounters with nature will charge us with tranquility allowing us to slow down our pace and enjoy the sun, birds, animals and plants. And when we open our eyes to its beauty and fully concentrate on our connection with nature, we will feel our whole being filled with reverence for its grandeur.

Today, more than ever, we need to slow down and appreciate that precious gift. Reconnecting with nature should become a priority in our daily lives. Excuses that we live in big cities are not acceptable because, even in our urban world, opportunities are still available. We have the city parks, where we can stroll along the alleys, sit on a bench or on the ground, listen to the songs of birds and gaze at blooming flowers, buzzing bees and fluffy clouds. If we want to be more active, we can play badminton, throw a boomerang or engage in another game. Outdoor activities among trees, grass and flowers will surely exhilarate us.

Our experiences will vary depending on the seasons. In spring, we can recharge by observing everything coming to life and blooming, under the joyful songs of birds. In summer, parks will provide us with shady cool greenery, while in autumn, we will be dazzled by the beauty of autumn with its bursting shades of yellow, red, brown and green and enjoy walking over the soft carpet of fallen leaves. Winter will enchant us with its silence, snowy landscape and the feeling of peace. Whatever the season, any interaction with nature will be recharging and refreshing, providing us with a good night's sleep and a lively spirit.

While parks offer opportunities for easy connection with nature, we should not give up on the possibilities for longer and more serious encounters. It is good idea to explore the options offered by the place where you live. Find out if there is a nearby mountain, a river, a nature reserve or a small mountain village that can be easily visited when you have a few days off. The possibilities are many; you just need to research and see which ones suit best your physical condition, desire and free time.

Regardless of the opportunities you have, let your periodic trips in nature be your priority. Plan walks, trips and visits that give you moments of relaxation and rejuvenation. If you are fortunate enough to have easy access to nature, take full advantage of it. Walk among the trees, hug a trunk if you feel like it or take the time to simply sit on the ground without any rush or making plans and just watch the flowers, trees and birds. Walk barefoot and feel the earth or grass under your feet. Lie down on the ground gazing at the clouds and the sky, and you will see how without any effort you will feel better. Every contact with the earth, whether just standing barefoot, lying on the ground or touching it, is a source of a magnetic force that will help you sense the power and peace of the planet Earth.

You should also plan longer stays in nature like a mountain or seaside holiday, a visit to a mountain village, a long hike or a picnic. Take every opportunity to detach yourself from the daily routine and slow down the rhythm far from the hustle and bustle of big cities. In summer and spring, enjoy the sunrises and sunsets, and then in the darkness of the night, let yourself be captivated by the vast sky and the glittering stars. If you are by the sea, take time to walk along the beach, watch the waves and listen to their sound. When in the mountains, immerse yourself in the greenness, the scent of trees, the fresh air and the songs of birds. These are things that will help you relax, find peace and feel refreshed.

If these activities seem challenging due to your health condition, don't lose hope. If you have a garden or a balcony, spend time outside when the weather is nice. Even short periods of exposure to light can make you feel better. If you don't have a garden or live in an industrialized area, you can enjoy the sight of a bouquet of fresh flowers or a blooming plant in your room, or listen to recordings of birdsongs, the sound of ocean waves or the buzzing of bees which can have a healing effect even when listened to on a recording. Videos of animals and nature's beauty can also raise your spirits and give you moments of joy.

Never stop seeking ways and opportunities to feel good and draw inspiration from the magnificence of our planet.

Your notes:

1-3 things to use in the future:

GRATITUDE

One practice that is worth including in everyone's daily life is gratitude. Though we may think it is simple and that we are generally grateful, the moment we try to do it regularly we quickly realize that it requires effort. If you look closely at the moments when you feel grateful, you may notice that you often take the good things for granted while dwelling on the things you don't have or miss. Gratitude helps us feel happy for anything that happens to us and for what we have, while its absence makes us blind to the good in our lives. To remind ourselves of the power of gratitude and all the things and people in our lives we should be grateful for, we celebrate January 11 as International Thank You Day.

The good news about gratitude is that, like with muscles, we can train and develop it, thus increasing the benefits associated with it on both physical and mental levels. When we approach life with gratitude, we are more resilient to stress, more accepting of negative experiences, we have a stronger belief and a more positive attitude. Perhaps that's why grateful people more easily go through difficulties and look at things in a brighter way.

In fact, gratitude is closely related to the positive attitude towards life. With such an attitude, even in the most difficult moments and situations, we can find something to be grateful for and thus change our perspective on it. Given its infinite benefits, it is crucial to cultivate gratitude in our daily lives – say "thank you" more often and pay attention to the things that happen to us. Every event carries a message for us and helps us grow. Sometimes, from the present, we don't always see the future consequences. Something that may seem one way today may have a completely different meaning and perception in the future. Well, I am far from the thought that we should adopt a perpetually positive outlook on life and be grateful for everything that happens to us, no matter how painful it may be at the moment. What I mean is to try and avoid getting stuck in the negative emotions and obstacles we encounter and notice the good things that each day brings us. If we fail noticing the good, we can never be grateful. Many of us say "thank you" mechanically or rarely. Just think how often you say or hear these words. I'm sure you know the answer – seldom. That's why it's worth trying to say "thank you" more often and truly contemplate the things in our lives for which we should be grateful.

You can start by choosing someone close to you and pay attention to the things they do for you over a few days and every time express your gratitude by saying "thank you." When I decided to start this practice, I chose my mother. In the first few days, it felt strange to notice all the things she was doing for me and express gratitude. It was like waking up to see how many of these things I take for granted without giving them a single thought. I realized that we were not accustomed to giving or even receiving thanks. No wonder, my mother was so surprised when I suddenly started saying "thank you" for things I used to overlook before. My advice is to try saying thank you for the small acts of kindness like the dinner someone made for you or the present you received or the care someone showed for you. While saying "thank you," focus on the feelings it brings, stop for a moment and look the other person in the eyes.

Perhaps after trying to thank someone for a few days, you may decide to expand the circle by including more people to express your gratitude to and, why not, turn it into your everyday practice.

To develop your sense of gratefulness, you can include the following practice in your daily life. For a month, every evening before going to bed, try to write down 5 things from the day you are grateful for. The idea here is not just to mechanically record them but to pause and feel the emotion associated with each event that made you (or should have made you) feel grateful. Maybe at first, this will seem difficult. Finding positive things when we are not used to noticing them is not an easy task. You don't have to try and find something big but simply focus on the events and occurrences of the day that made you feel good. If even that seems difficult at first, you can try to be grateful that your needs were met, that you had food or managed to get some sleep, that someone smiled at you or said something nice to you, or even for seeing a blooming flower. The fact that you have shelter and something to eat, and you have woken up to live one more day on Earth is enough reason to be grateful. Let your thoughts flow, and you will discover that you have much more than 5 things from the day to be thankful for. Over time, you will start noticing more and more easily the beautiful moments and events that deserve your gratitude.

This is one of the things that hold an important place in my life. Since I've been practicing it, I became aware of how often we take the victim position, complaining about life and all the troubles, while rarely appreciating what we have and the positive events in our lives. I can't hide that sometimes I, too, fall into ingratitude and see myself as a victim, complaining and being dissatisfied with the course of events. Fortunately, at some point, I hear an inner voice whispering to me to stop all that and look with gratitude at what I have and everything that happens to me. Next, I realize that by taking the victim approach, I, unconsciously, actually become one and do my best to turn my thoughts to the things I am blessed with.

This practice helps us shift the focus from what we lack to what we have and prevents us from comparing ourselves to others which inevitably makes us feel better, more confident and happier.

Remember that any approach and practice can be changed according to your needs. In case writing down 5 positive things in the evening seems impossible and unacceptable to you, you can try to only mentally note a few things from the day that you are grateful for. As with writing them down, it is particularly important to take your time to feel the emotion of the events and relive the joy.

If even this turns out unsuccessful, but you love meditating, you can experiment and include gratitude as part of it. While doing your meditation, you can focus on 1-3 things you are grateful for. This approach is actually my favourite and it helps me a lot, especially in situations when I am in a bad mood or feel low. By turning to gratitude, I always manage to change my negative perspective.

Try bravely and never stop being grateful. Even in the darkest moments of life, there is something to be grateful for. And when we learn to notice the good things, they actually start happening to us more and more often.

Your notes:

1-3 things to use in the future:

FORGIVENESS

Forgiveness is an integral part of gratitude. As we go through life, each of us accumulates grievances, betrayals and disappointments. Even if we don't want it, the bitterness they leave often remains within us for a long time. A word of offense or a daily confrontation can emotionally unsettle many of us and make us relive the situation and the pain for hours and days. For those who are more sensitive and vulnerable like me, confrontation and offense can have a much stronger effect. That's why forgiveness is so important to me. It helps me cleanse my soul and free myself from the pain caused by someone else's words or actions.

I divide forgiveness into two main categories: forgiveness towards oneself and forgiveness towards others. Forgiveness towards oneself is fundamental. It is not only a testament to the love we have for ourselves but also a foundation for our healthy existence. I believe each of us has something to forgive ourselves for. If you think you are an exception, you are certainly mistaken.

Work on self-forgiveness takes time. You can begin by writing a letter to yourself seeking forgiveness for past situations and actions for which you blamed yourself and felt regret. Share your disappointment, pain and self-accusations, and then try to ask for and give forgiveness to yourself.

Even if you are reluctant, make an effort and do this practice. It helped me realize that I have always wanted more and more from myself, taking no rest even when I needed it and that I have often blamed myself unjustly or put myself in the background as if I loved myself less than I loved others. Perhaps the most crucial realization for me was that whatever I did, wherever I was, it was never enough; there was always someone better than me and new things to learn and do. Turning to myself and recalling the situations where I have been harsh on myself, I realized that I need to treat myself with more compassion, understanding and love.

Another way to perform this act of self-forgiveness is by standing in front of the mirror, looking into your own eyes and reflecting on the things which weigh on your conscience. Say them out loud while still gazing into your eyes. Finally, say that you forgive yourself. Pay attention to the emotions and thoughts that arise in that moment and write them down in your journal.

Forgiveness towards others can be more complex and even painful. That's why, right from the beginning, I want to clarify that some situations may be challenging to handle on your own and may require help from a specialist. When I talk about forgiveness towards others, I mean trivial situations and minor confrontations that, more or less, affect our emotional state. Dealing with such emotions is not an easy job. When I am overwhelmed by strong emotions, I first ask myself whether they belong to me. Often the answer is somehow surprising: they don't. Becoming aware of this fact helps me understand those emotions and let them go.

To forgive, you need to put yourself in the other person's shoes and try to imagine the reasons behind their actions, reminding yourself that people who have been hurt often hurt others. By causing pain to other people, they are actually trying to escape from their own pain. Understanding this sometimes helps to clear the offense more easily. Remember that we have no control over others and their perceptions but we can take control over ourselves and our feelings, so it's worth working on that.

When we forgive, the aim is not to love and accept the other person but to free ourselves from their influence. During this process, however, we may change our attitude towards them many times and even feel compassion. Of course, it all depends on the type of offense or disappointment and their degree. When I try to forgive, I want to purify my soul and shed the burden of someone else's actions while also freeing my own energy. Regardless of your motives, remember that when you forgive, you do it for yourselves, not the other person, as you want to feel better and move forward.

There are situations we can easily handle but there are also those where we cannot shake off our emotions no matter how many times we repeat to ourselves that the problem and blame are not ours. Sometimes it is really difficult to forgive and move on. Nevertheless, don't give up! Have love for yourselves and set free from your anger and negative emotions towards others. Don't regard it as a miracle; forgiveness simply requires self-work, which sometimes can take longer.

A few events from the past still perturb me even though it's been years since then, but thanks to my efforts, I am now able to accept what happened and feel mainly empathy for those who have hurt me while struggling with their own problems and trying to fill their own void.

The topic is extensive, and surely everyone has enough experience and situations that call for forgiveness. You can start by choosing a recent event that still occupies your thoughts or making a list of people you want to forgive. Go slowly through this list, gradually freeing yourself from the burden you carry in your heart. With time, you will undoubtedly feel the soul-healing effect of genuine forgiveness.

<u>Your notes</u>:

<u>1-3 things to use in the future</u>:

LOVE

As the famous song goes "All you need is love!"

Love is the driving force in life and it is obvious why so many songs and movies have been dedicated to it. You might be surprised that I included love as a separate practice when it seems so natural to love. Well, I think that its significance and main place in our lives makes it worth this special attention as a separate practice.

In this chapter, the focus is on self-love, without excluding love for all living beings. Why self-love? Primarily because we are the most important person to ourselves. Friends around us may come and go but until the end of our earthly journey, we will be with ourselves. We are our best friend and most loyal companion but, unfortunately, we sometimes become our worst enemy. That's why it's essential to love ourselves and develop that love because, as long as we live, we have ourselves.

However, things in real life are different. Instead of loving ourselves, we are overly demanding. Instead of treating ourselves with love and compassion in times of failure and setbacks, we are critical and blameful. We often console our friends for their failures but seldom treat ourselves with the same sympathy and understanding.

There are various practices that aim to help us love and accept ourselves as we are. One of my favourites is that of Louise Hay. I strongly advise you to include it in your daily routine or at least try it for 21 days. The practice is extremely simple – all you have to do is stand in front of the mirror, look deep into your eyes and say "I love you." Yes, you need to say it out loud, while looking into your eyes, not just think it. Repeat this practice every day, as many times as you want and at any time. You may be surprised to find that for some people it's not as easy as it seems to express love for themselves. Even if you are one of those who find it difficult, don't give up but keep going. You can only gain more love for yourself. If, however, it's very challenging for you to say to your reflection "I love you," you can try saying that you intend to love yourself or that you are on the path to loving yourself. This will certainly help you, too; with time, it will become easier for you to express self-love.

Since this practice works on a deep emotional level, it is not unlikely that it might evoke strong emotions. Don't worry! Welcome these emotions with curiosity and acceptance. It's also a good idea to write them down. When the 21 days are over, assess the results and then decide whether you want to continue with the practice. If you choose to go on, be confident and don't give up. On the other hand, if you decide that you don't like the practice or don't want to continue further, you can still occasionally say to yourself in front of the mirror that you love yourself. Surely, you will feel better afterward.

In any case, try to pay attention to the way you talk to yourself and the kind of language you use, and recognize the voice of criticism. Be your own best friend with whom you only speak with understanding, compassion and love.

Your notes:

1-3 things to use in the future:

As a next step in strengthening your love for yourself, you can do another interesting exercise. Take some time to reflect on the things you are grateful for about your body and the things you love and appreciate about yourself. Then, write a letter to yourself expressing your love, listing the things you are thankful for about your body, soul and mind. Once you're ready, read the letter and see how many things you love about yourself which also call for your gratitude.

You can take it a step further by including in the list the things you don't like about yourself but try to approach them with understanding, compassion and acceptance. Just like in the previous exercise, this practice involves working with emotions, so it might bring up some forgotten feelings and, if you feel like it, you can write down the emotions they have triggered.

Your notes:

1-3 things to use in the future:

Another exercise you can try is to create two lists – one for the things that are exceptionally important to you and another for the things that are absolutely unimportant. Among the things that are exceptionally important to me, for example, are the need to rest and listen to my body. This means that no matter how much I want do jogging, I must recognize the signals of my body and engage in another sport that brings me pleasure without feeling in pain or being exhausted. By saying this, I don't mean that you should exclude jogging from your daily life; just listen to your body and approach things strictly individually, choosing what gives you joy and satisfaction.

The list of my "categorical no's" defines my boundaries. It includes the decision not to allow anyone to treat me poorly or insult me and never compare myself to others. It doesn't mean that I should not admire and respect the efforts and achievements of other people. When I say comparing to others, I mean engaging in a negative self-dialogue that makes me feel inferior.

Once you know the things that are absolutely important for you and those that are not, you can focus on bringing more important things into your life and reducing the unimportant ones. By taking care of yourself, you are actually showing that you matter. Remember that the goal is to love yourself unconditionally, regardless of all your flaws. And what is a flaw? What someone finds annoying and negative in you may be the most attractive feature to someone else. If you don't like something about yourself, accept it and work on improving it because you want to, but still love yourself.

Whichever practice you choose, when you direct your efforts towards yourself, the results will come, sooner or later. You will find that you start valuing and loving yourself more and that it is easier to establish your personal boundaries and stand up for them. Say the difficult "no" when you have to, and don't forget that saying "yes" sometimes means neglecting yourself in favour of someone else. This includes both your personal and professional life. For example, a "No" at your workplace means assessing that an extra task will come too much to you, and saying openly that despite your desire, you can't take it on.

When self-love is absent, we tend to prioritize the desires and needs of others over our own, even in cases where this could harm us. Consider how many times you've simply agreed to go out or do something, without really wanting it or feeling tired and stressed, just because someone asked you to. I've been in that position many times – agreeing to do something just because I'm afraid to say ‚no' and then regretting it.

So, you'd better listen to your body and heart before saying "Yes" or "No". When self-love leads us, we treat ourselves with compassion and communicate our desires without fear.

It is essential to know first what is good for us if we want to stand up for it and establish our boundaries. For this purpose, you can try another exercise that is very short and simple. You just have to reflect on the important things that you are unwilling to make compromises about since this may affect your health, mood or emotions. My personal boundaries include not allowing others to insult me, getting enough sleep, listening to my body and taking a break when I feel tired or stressed at work.

You will definitely notice that when you love yourself, your love for others increases, too. This applies to both close friends and family as well as to complete strangers. What's more, the love others have for you can also grow. And that's normal because people seem to sense when we love ourselves and show that love.

After you have perfected self-love, you can move on to love for others. First of all, refrain from criticizing and judging others. Adopt the idea that each person does their best in every moment. Every decision or action is based on personal experiences and the environment we live in. Every criticism or judgment is based on our subjective understanding and perception of things, which may be entirely unacceptable or different from those of others. In fact, we tend to hate other people's traits we ourselves possess and that's exactly why we see them. When you stop judging others, you'll notice how your relationships with them improve and how easier it is to see the good in them and find qualities to admire. Besides, the time that we would otherwise waste discussing other people's lives and decisions can be used for our own development and well-being.

I will conclude the Love chapter with the necessity of daily acts of kindness and help towards others. It's a common truth that when a person does good it has a positive effect on them and they feel better. This is entirely natural because we are social beings and need other people to survive. When a friend or loved one suffers or goes through a difficult period, it affects us too, and vice versa, their joy charges us positively. In addition, the feeling that we have helped someone, cheered them up or just made them smile brings an internal sense of fulfilment, the satisfaction that we have contributed to this world. After all, we all want to make it a better place.

Try to be open, compassionate and responsive to people. Don't forget that tomorrow you might be in the same situation. Be kind and helpful whenever possible. Sometimes even a smile can make someone's day. One kind word or a little help may be priceless. Open your heart! It will bring you only satisfaction, and people will feel your love.

<u>Your notes</u>:

<u>1-3 things to use in the future</u>:

EFT AND VISUALIZATION

The Emotional Freedom Technique (EFT) was created in 1990 by Gary Craig. This extremely simple technique is based on the Chinese medicine understanding that the human body has energy meridians through which our energy flows. In EFT, specific points located on these meridians are tapped with the fingertips in a particular sequence. The technique is used to resolve various emotional and psychological issues, as well as alleviate physical pain. It can be used for both acute and chronic conditions as many times as you wish. For acute conditions, you can do EFT until you feel relief, and for chronic conditions, you can use it for longer periods.

When I started doing EFT, I had many issues to work on, so I made a list of them with the intensity of each one. While working consistently on each issue, I noted whether the intensity changed. Later on, I used EFT only when needed, for e.g., to mitigate a particular emotion, physical pain or psychological state.

Currently, there are various versions of EFT regarding which points to tap and in what sequence. I will focus on the technique that I use without claiming it to be exhaustive.

Here is how the technique works:

1. Initially, take a deep breath and identify the issue you will be working on and its intensity on a scale from 1 to 10, where 10 is the highest intensity.
2. Formulate an affirmation based on the issue, using the template: "Even though [**name the problem**], I deeply and sincerely accept and love myself."
3. It is essential to describe the problem in as much detail as possible, as well as its cause. For example, if you feel anxious and worried, instead of using a general statement like "Even though I feel anxious, I deeply and sincerely accept and love

myself," it's better to identify what exactly causes your anxiety and include the explanation in the core affirmation. So, the correct affirmation example would be: "Even though I feel anxious because of the presentation I have to give, I deeply and sincerely accept and love myself."

4. After creating the affirmation, move on to tapping the points in the following sequence: Start with the so-called "karate point," located on the outer edge of your hand, beginning from the base of your little finger and extending to your wrist. Tap the "karate point" with the fingers of your other hand, while repeating the core affirmation three times.

5. After stating the core affirmation, proceed by voicing the feelings that this state arouses as you tap the following points:

    -   The point where the inner eyebrow begins (both sides) – using one or both hands
    -   The outside of the eyes (both sides)
    -   Under the eyes (both sides)
    -   Under the nose
    -   Chin (the indention)
    -   Collarbone (3 inches under it)
    -   Underarm (about 4 inches below the armpit)
    -   Top of head

An example tapping sequence would go like this:

-   Tap the inner eyebrow and say: "I'm very worried about this presentation."
-   Tap the outer side of the eyes and say: "I feel my whole body tensing up."
-   Tap under the eyes and say: "My thoughts are solely focused on this and I'm not thinking about anything else."
-   Tap under the nose and say: "My palms are getting sweaty."

- Tap the chin and say: "Can I handle speaking in front of so many people?"
- Tap under the collarbone and say: "I can't cope with that."
- Tap the underarm and say: "I won't be able to say anything."
- Tap the top of your head and say: "My anxiety is overwhelming."

All these examples are aimed at giving you an idea of how to perform the technique. When tapping each point, it's good to say spontaneously your thoughts. Allow yourself to feel the emotions, and try to sense what is bothering you. After going through all the points, and expressing the things that you are worried about, move on to the next round, which consists of positive and encouraging statements repeated with each tap. For example, such statements could be: "I am full of strength," "I am confident and will handle it with ease," etc., pronounced aloud while you are following the sequence points mentioned earlier. Finish by tapping the top of the head and finally take a deep breath. Check the intensity level of the emotion after applying the technique. If the level is still high, you can repeat the technique again. Sometimes, when working on a stronger emotion, you may find that even after applying the technique, the intensity has not decreased or it may even have increased. It's quite possible if you are very susceptible to this emotion. In such cases, you just need to continue working on it. When the intensity level of the emotion drops below 3, you can stop.

However, it's also possible that while the emotion you are working on decreases, another one arises. In this case, you will have to address the new one, too.

The possibilities are many; experiment and try the technique in different situations to see if it works for you. Although it is important to verbalize the affirmations during the technique, if that's not possible, you can say them silently in your mind while tapping the points. Often, even tapping without specific affirmations can have a positive effect.

If you want to learn more about EFT, you can read a book on the topic or search the Internet for info and apps that offer various practices related to this subject.

<u>Your notes</u>:

<u>1-3 things to use in the future</u>:

Another practice worth trying in your daily life is visualization. The practice is very easy to perform, but the results are impressing. It is based on a detailed mental representation of what you want to achieve.

For visualizations you have to take some time and be alone with yourself. Choose an area or goal to work on. For example, answer the question of what you want to achieve or where and what changes you want to see. Write down your desire or the goal that you want to achieve as if it has already happened. Don't write as if you're not sure it's going to happen nor use the future tense. After writing down your goal, close your eyes and try to imagine it in a way that it has already happened. It's important to use all your senses when visualizing. This would mean imagining the situation as vividly as possible, how you would feel, what smells you would smell and what sounds you would hear. Take your time, don't rush to finish but really immerse yourself in what you're visualizing. Pay attention to the colors you see, the sounds and the smells. Try to make the visualization as real as possible. Approach it like it's something that's bound to happen and don't ask yourself how. This is not important, your focus should be on how you would feel if your wish has already come true. When visualizing, it is also good to imagine the positive effect of what you dream on other people – our dreams should benefit them, too. Take your time and pay attention to all details and emotions it evokes. When you are ready, open your eyes. How do you feel?

One session is not enough and you should go on with visualization practice for some time perfecting your ability to imagine yourself as living in the desired reality and your goals as already achieved.

Your notes:

1-3 things to use in the future:

EXTERNAL ENVIRONMENT

Amidst all the changes and efforts you make to feel better, it is essential to pay attention to the environment in which you live and the people you surround yourself with.

To begin, take stock of all the available external and internal resources at your disposal. By resources, I mean the people, things and activities that help you feel better. Pay special attention to those that make you feel supported, understood and valued. Everyone needs support and friends who lift them up and inspire confidence in their abilities. Therefore, when considering your resources and deciding who is a true friend, the first question to answer should be whether the contacts with those people make you feel better. Can you openly share your dreams with them and receive support and understanding, or it's rather you meet misunderstanding and discouragement? If during this assessment, you realize that there are people who burden you and make you feel worse, it is necessary to consider whether they are true friends or you'd better avoid their company. This assessment will help you increase the presence of those people in your life who have a positive impact on you and give you wings, rather than cut them down. Show them that you value them and their opinions, maintain contact with them and invest emotionally in your friendships.

Remember that while we cannot choose our parents, we are responsible for our friendships and the people we surround ourselves with.

Reflecting on the qualities and activities that are your external and internal resources will help you realize what you love doing that helps you feel better. Once you have identified them, try to incorporate them into your daily life. Such activities could be meditation, yoga, spending time in nature, and so on.

If you find that you lack supporting resources, direct your attention towards bringing such into your life. Humor and laughter should undoubtedly occupy an important place among your resources because their benefits are immense. Personally, I have always wondered at how much children laugh, and how as we grow older the portion of laughter seems to decrease. I can't explain why this happens, whether with time we embrace the solemn role of adults and laugh rarely, or pressed by life's challenges, we unconsciously forget to laugh. Sometimes the things that used to make us laugh to tears, now seem quite ordinary or even dull and tedious. To change our approach to laughter, we need to make an effort to see the funny side of things and not take ourselves too seriously. The easiest practice to bring more laughter into our daily lives is to watch comedy movies, sketches or videos. Look for the funny in every situation, approach yourself with self-irony and try to laugh. Even if it's difficult at first, with time it will become easier and bring more joy to your life.

Another exercise you can do is to identify the things that burden you the most and have a negative influence on you. Next you should either get rid of this resource or at least do something to reduce its presence and impact. For example, you might decide to seek help or delegate some tasks to others, and so on. A good piece of advice here is to maintain a positive inner dialogue and be inventive. In my case the reflctions on this issue helped me realize that when I feel overwhelmed by tasks and commitments, I can become quite tense and anxious. To help myself in such situations, it's important for me to take more breaks which calms me down and helps me feel better and more confident. I've realized that when I'm tired and stressed, I tend to approach a situation with much more negativity and feel worse. In such cases, admitting that I'm tired and need a break, I approach myself with compassion and understanding and try to avoid any overreacting.

To confine the impact of the external environment, you can do something else – get rid of old and unnecessary things. I know this idea may be scaring at first, but I can assure you that hoarding always has a deleterious effect on all levels of our personal and social lives, while decluttering our homes can play an extremely positive role, freeing us both physically and psychologically. The feeling after releasing unnecessary things is similar to that of liberation, besides we can help those in need or just make other people happy.

You can start with the clothes and shoes you don't wear but are in good condition. If you find it difficult to part with some of your items, don't force yourself; start with one or two things. Establish rules for parting will make your task easier, for example, a piece of clothing you haven't worn or used in the last three years or something that no longer fits you. Once you've decided to let it go, don't rush to throw it directly in the trash. Assess its condition and decide whether you can donate it to someone in need or take it to a used clothes or shoes container. There are many options, so you can always choose the most acceptable for you.

Your notes:

1-3 things to use in the future:

OTHER PRACTICES

So far, I have tried to present to you the most important practices to me. Certainly, this list is not exhaustive. New practices constantly emerge and can also be included in the list. Perhaps there are ones that you yourselves use and find helpful.

Among the new practices I'd like to mention are energy medicine and energy yoga. In the field of energy medicine, the work of Donna Eden stands out, aiming to normalize and balance body energy and to ensure its smooth and unrestricted flow. If this is an area of interest to you, you can search the Internet for feature videos, covering energy exercises for joy and happiness.

Another practice is the emotional code by Bradley Nelson, which is used to release past emotions that we have not let go of.

Muscle relaxation is another technique where specific muscle groups are sequentially tensed and then relaxed. This practice is suitable for releasing accumulated tension at the end of the day or after stressful situations. Regular massage can also have a positive impact on our bodies and help release tension.

If there are other practices that you like, you can include those, too, in your daily life. Remember that whatever practice you choose, it should not make you feel stressed but rather support your well-being. Be creative and organize your daily routine in such a way that you always have some free time for yourself.

Your notes:

1-3 things to use in the future:

YOUR PERSONAL PRACTICES

After going through the different practices and noting those you want to include in your daily life, it's time to review your notes for each practice and create a visually clear list of the areas you want to work on and the time you are willing to allocate to each.

As a first step, you can complete the following table.

PRACTICE	FREQUENCY

In the frequency column, indicate how often you want to use each practice. For example, if you want to incorporate meditation into your daily life, you may want the frequency to be every morning or both morning and evening. If you want to include positive affirmations, you may want the frequency to be daily.

When filling in the table, be realistic and consider your current state and real possibilities. Listen to your body and don't be overly ambitious. The goal is not to do all practices every day and feel stressed but to choose those that resonate best with you. Start with fewer activities and increase them over time if you like. Remember that less but more consistent is better as it will prevent you from feeling it like a burden and giving up on everything at once. Of course, you can always modify the practices and their frequency.

You can also choose which practices to include in your morning routine and how much time to allocate to each. For example, my morning ritual includes meditation, positive affirmations and gratitude. Occasionally, I add Emotional Freedom Technique (EFT) and visualization.

Once you have determined the practices and their frequency, you can take another step forward by creating a daily-weekly-monthly schedule using the following table.

EVERY DAY	WEEKLY	MONTHLY
Morning		
Noon		

Evening		

In the first column, enter the practices you want to perform every day, such as meditation, breathing exercises, etc. Be more specific if it helps and divide them throughout the day, as shown in the table – morning, noon, evening.

In the weekly column, write the practices you want to use throughout the week. For instance, this could include sports and other physical activities. Similar to the previous column, you can be more specific and specify on which day of the week you want to do each practice.

In the last column, include the practices you want to incorporate on a monthly basis – for example, spending time in nature, etc., or simply review what you've been doing so far, what is the effect and whether you need to make adjustments to get better results.

As with everything so far, remember that you are the only one who knows what's best for you, so keep following your inner voice and intuition.

Once the table is filled out, you have a ready plan for incorporating these practices into your daily life. You can print it out and place it somewhere visible which will facilitate you in following it.

PRIORITY-AWARENESS

The last chapter of the Practices is focused on becoming aware of our priorities. Perhaps this isn't precisely a practice but rather a necessary self-assessment to help us develop our potential and live in sync with our desires and feelings.

I feel the need to pay special attention to this practice because in today's fast-paced world, opportunities to truly understand ourselves and figure out what we want from life seem limited. In such an environment, it's easy to go with the flow and live a life that may not align with our true selves but conforms to societal expectations and norms like finishing school, getting a job, starting a family, raising children, retiring and eventually concluding our lives. This may be so far from the essence of life, failing to reflect how diverse we are as individuals, each with different potentials and missions on this planet.

I firmly believe that to live mindfully and fulfil our potential, we need to turn inward, become aware of what makes us happy and what we want from life. By becoming aware of our desires, it will be easier for us to find the path to achieving our dreams and strive for them.

Of course, working on ourselves requires time and the willingness to explore. The goal is to examine each area of our life that is significant to us and try to answer questions like: What do we want in that sphere? Why is it important to us? What actions can we take to achieve our dreams, and what we are not willing to take? Reviewing different aspects of life will help us identify our priorities and then work for their realization[7]. This perspective will enable us to examine our lives, recognize the areas where we want to make changes and what we want to accomplish. It will also help us ponder the contributions we want to make to life and the ways to achieve them.

The categorization provided below is an example, so you can modify it to resonate best with you. For instance, if you feel there are too many spheres and only two of them are important to you, then focus on these two. The idea is that by working on yourself, you can truly become aware of the most important things for you and the ways to achieve them.

---

[7] If interested you can look at Jon and Missy Butcher Lifebook program

Education

Education encompasses both formal education obtained in schools or universities and any additional self-improvement and development, including learning a foreign language or acquiring new skills. To determine your priorities in this area, you need to reflect on whether your education and occupation align with your dreams. Is it essential for you to grow and acquire new knowledge? Do you need or just want to learn a new language or obtain new skills? Focus on the following questions:

- Do I enjoy learning new things?
- Is there something I want to learn that excites me?
- Do I need new skills and knowledge to achieve my professional development goals?
- What is the timeframe for accomplishing these goals? Do I want to achieve them now, or can they wait and be pursued in the future?

When answering these questions and contemplating this area, don't think about how you would cope with it or how much effort it might cost you. Initially, the questions and contemplation aim to define your priorities. Only then can you consider the actions you will take, depending on what you want to achieve and when. For example, you may decide to enroll in a new course and start it as soon as possible, or do some specialization.

To take any actions, we need motivation, and what greater motivation than realizing that we want to do it because it is important to us.

<u>Your notes</u>:

<u>Priorities in this sphere</u>:

Profession

Work occupies a significant place in our daily lives. In fact, the greater part of our days is taken up by work. It is therefore essential to find joy and satisfaction in what we do for a living. Unfortunately, a large number of people dislike their jobs or encounter problems at their workplace (with colleagues or bosses), and as a result, they do their jobs with reluctance. If that's the case, it's very difficult for us to simply ignore it because when such a great part of our time is dedicated to a particular job, the way we feel there and the emotions we experience impact other areas of our life.

That's why it's crucial to take our jobs seriously and answer the following questions:

- Does my job give me satisfaction?
- Am I doing what I desire?
- Do I have any unfulfilled dreams regarding the kind of job I would like to do or the things I have longed to achieve?
- What do I enjoy doing?
- Do I have any hobbies or activities that bring me joy and what are they?
- If I don't feel happy with what I'm currently doing, what steps can I take to change this situation?
- What matters to me in my job – being happy and satisfied, having good colleagues, professional development, job security, good earnings, fixed working hours or flexible working hours?
- Is it important for me to have contact with people?
- Do I like facing new challenges?

These are only example questions, and once you decide to shed light on your professional life and what makes you happy, you can certainly expand that list.

In any case, try to establish clarity on the following:

- Whether you are satisfied with your current job
- Whether you have secret dreams or you would be better suited to another field, often considered a hobby
- Your job priorities
- If there's something you can do to feel better

This is a serious process and may take some time. Don't worry. The idea is once you have determined where you stand regarding your job and what your priorities are, you can take the necessary actions.

Even if you realize that you are not satisfied with your job but at the same time you don't want to seek new professional challenges, there is always the possibility to change your attitude and approach to what you are currently doing. Reflect on the contribution of your job and who benefits from it. Being aware that you are doing something that is good for the others can have a positive effect. For example, I myself like to imagine that my work in a certain field helps a particular group of people. This mindset keeps me going, even in cases when someone asks me some seemingly tedious questions. By putting myself in the shoes of the other person and imagining how I would feel if I received a negative response, I become more cooperative and do my best to craft my answer.

It is precisely this change in our attitude towards our job and responsibilities that alters our reaction to tasks we originally found boring and routine.

Once you have determined your priorities, consider how you can realize them and write down your ideas below.

Your notes:

Priorities in this sphere:

Friendship

Friendship is another sphere worth looking into to examine the relationships we build with other people. Again, here it's essential to take time for ourselves and reflect on the significance of friendship in our lives. Answering the questions below will certainly help with that:

- Do you have many friends?
- Do you make friends easily?
- Do you enjoy spending time with your friends?
- How often do you see your friends?
- How important is friendship to you?
- Do you share your problems with your friends?
- Do you seek advice and help from your friends?
- What is important to you in a friendship?
- Who are your friends?
- Are your friendships mutual?
- Do you do enough to maintain your friendships?

The answers to these questions would help you realize what you value in a friendship, what expectations you have and what you are willing to give. The idea is that once you figure out what is important to you in a specific area of your life, it becomes easier to act in accordance with your priorities. For example, if you realize that friendship is an important part of your inner world, it's essential to maintain and develop your relationships – call friends more often, spend more time with them, organise common activities etc. Think of a friendship as a flower that requires care, time and effort. No matter how much you value someone as a friend, if your contacts with them are rare they will become less enjoyable and positive and your friendship will weaken over time.

To me this sphere comprises not only friendship but all interactions we have with people on a daily basis. To understand their significance for you, consider whether you enjoy contacting people and talking to strangers. Do these contacts recharge you or you get tired from socializing and prefer to be alone? What is essential to you regarding your relationships with others? The purpose of these questions is to help you get to know yourself better and understand the importance of social connections for you so that you can develop and improve them if needed.

Your notes:

Priorities in this sphere:

Health

Including health among personal priorities may seem strange, considering that, in one way or another, the whole book is dedicated to health. The idea of this separate chapter is to help you gain clarity on what you desire regarding your health, your priorities and how motivated you are to achieve them.

We all attribute different meaning to being healthy. For some, it is merely the absence of certain symptoms. For others it's having energy, and for others still, it's healing from a serious illness, and so on. Whatever the implied meaning, we can all unanimously agree that health is the greatest wealth we possess. Only when we are healthy can we fully enjoy life and strive to achieve our dreams.

To understand the meaning and importance of health for yourselves, it is necessary to set aside some time for reflection. Use the questions below as a foundation for contemplation and feel free to supplement the list with more:

- What does health mean for you?
- How important is it for you to be healthy?
- What health state do you want to achieve?
- What are you willing to do to be healthy?
- Who do you want to be healthy for?
- Do you believe it's normal to feel worse and get sicker with age?
- Do you think that health is largely genetically determined?

When pondering this sphere, don't forget that, in one way or another, health underlies every other aspect of life, as only in good physical, emotional and mental health can you pursue your other priorities.

I can truly say that for me health is my utmost personal priority. Realizing that only when I feel well and healthy can I achieve my dreams and be of help to the people I love and those around me has helped me introduce all the changes in my life without feeling burdened. When you know where you don't want to end up and what you strive for, it becomes much easier to make changes that may seem difficult and unattainable at first.

That's why I advise you not to skip this part but give it the necessary time and attention. It will not only help you follow the practices you've chosen but also provide you with strength and awareness in stressful situations and when making your everyday choices.

Your notes:

Priorities in this sphere:

Family

In this sphere you can include everyone that you see as part of your family. It could be your partner or spouse, your children or parents, siblings or other relatives. The number doesn't matter and can be as few as two or much larger, including brothers, sisters and other relatives.

Once you've identified the people who represent your family, it's necessary to understand the significance of each one of them to you. Only when we realize someone's importance to us can we consciously dedicate our time and attention to them.

As a starting point, try to answer the question "What role does family play in my life?" To me, for example, family is a sense of belonging, a unit bound by common goals; it is supporting each other in difficulties and sharing joy in success and progress.

Then focus on the following questions:

- What emotions does my family give me?
- Do I feel understood and loved by my family?
- What is the atmosphere in the family?
- Does spending time with my family recharge me or I feel misunderstood, tense or unnecessary?
- Do I look forward to coming home to my family after a difficult and tiring workday?
- Do I enjoy spending my free time with my family?
- Do I allocate enough time to my close people?
- Do they know how important they are to me?
- Do I show my feelings and emotions to my loved ones?
- Do I provide assistance to them when needed?
- What do I expect from my family?
- What does family mean to me and what am I willing to do for it?

You can certainly add more questions to the list related to the family topic. Examine your answers. They will surely help you understand how your family functions at the moment and its significance for you. Reflect on what you want your family to be like and on your priorities in this sphere. This will help you take the right actions to align yourself with your established priorities.

For instance, reflecting on this helped me become aware of the immense importance of my family for my emotional and mental well-being. I realized that my family is the harbor I turn to when facing work and health problems, and they are the people I feel closest to my heart. And though I love and cherish them, I shouldn't take them for granted, but give them my time and attention in line with my priorities.

Your notes:

Priorities in this sphere:

Personal life

Some of you may think that I have already covered this subject in the family section. Well, it's partially true but in Personal life I'd like to dwell on the things that bring you joy and occupy your personal free time, like hobbies, intimate relationships, and everything that is important to you.

If you're currently not in a relationship, I advise you to take some time, nonetheless, and think about what you expect from a partner, what your understanding of a mutual relationship is, what your boundaries are and what you wouldn't tolerate in a relationship. To get a comprehensive idea of your outlook on this sphere, focus on questions like:

- What is the role of a partner in your life?
- What significance do you give to your intimate relationships?
- How do you feel in this relationship, or if you're not in a relationship, how would you like to feel?
- Do you feel that the relationship helps you grow and brings out the best in you?
- How do your relationship dynamics affect your well-being?
- Do you feel understood?
- How would you be happier – alone or in this relationship?
- How important are intimate relationships to you?
- Do you openly communicate things that make you happy and those that hurt you?
- Do you openly discuss conflicts?
- Have you clearly communicated your boundaries and does your partner respect them?

Include any other questions that would help you realize the significance of your personal relationships and their role in your life. Apart from partner relationships, this sphere encompasses other aspects and priorities of your personal life that also deserve some reflection. For me, finding meaning and purpose in life definitely falls within this sphere.

To address this, answer the following questions:

- What are your goals in life?
- What is most important to you in life?
- What would you like to achieve?
- What would bring you the greatest joy and satisfaction?
- What do you enjoy doing in your free time?
- What activities inspire you?

Finding a life purpose is of immense importance to each one of us. Sooner or later, we all reach the point of questioning ourselves whether the things we do have meaning. Life's purpose varies greatly for each individual. For some, it might be accumulating wealth, for others, it's achieving fame and recognition, some might want to grow and excel in their profession, while others aim to build a loving family, raise healthy and good children and so on. It's possible to have more than one purpose. Looking at it this way, the purposes somewhat or greatly overlap with the priorities defined in each of the previous spheres, which can help you set your personal goals.

Ask questions and reflect on the answers to see what are the most important things to you in life. Just as in the previous spheres, when we know what we deeply desire, we can plan our actions to achieve it. With a clear idea and daily small steps towards its realization, we will easily fulfill our goal.

Your notes:

Priorities in this sphere:

APPENDIX FOR IDENTIFYING PRIORITIES AND ACTIONS

After reviewing each of the 6 main spheres and determining your priorities, it's time to outline the key actions you should take in order to achieve and live in sync with them.

For this purpose, use the notes after each chapter where you've identified your priorities and transfer them to the table below.

Against each priority, write the regular actions you want to take to align your life with them.

Priorities	Actions
1. Education	
2. Profession	
3. Friendship	
4. Health	

5. Family	
6. Personal Life	

The above table will be your guide, so that day by day you come closer to the set goals in harmony with your current priorities. With this we are at the end of our common journey. Congratulations for all your efforts and introspection. I hope that the work you've done so far will help you clearly define your actions and start incorporating them into your daily life. I strongly believe it won't be long before you pick the fruits of your labor.

CLOSING REMARKS

Dear reader, thank you for joining me in this deeply personal journey. I sincerely hope it has been helpful to you and that, at the end of it, you feel more confident and hopeful about changing your life. Knowledge is power and, when armed with the right tools, we gain courage and understand that we are not helpless.

Throughout our shared experience, you had the chance to look into various aspects of your existence, define your priorities and identify the necessary actions for their achievement. I believe you feel uplifted, stronger and filled with hope about the days to come. Step confidently on your path and believe that you will succeed.

Be patient and loving to yourself and the world. Never lose faith that after every storm the sun shines brighter and, sooner or later, it will shine for you, too.

I love you, and may the light illuminate your path!

ACKNOWLEDGEMENTS

I'd like to thank my loved ones and the teachers by my side without whom this book would not have become a reality. I give my thanks to my dear son, Nikolai, for being the light and joy in my life and to my parents and my sister, for being there for me in joy and sorrow. My infinite gratitude to my mother for her patience, support and assistance in my hardest moments. A big thank you to Karin Enders for being my mentor and healer during a time when I needed it most, for directing me to the information I needed, recommending books and offering endless hours of compassion, empathy and encouragement. My gratitude is boundless!

Endless thanks to Anthony William (Medical Medium) for the invaluable information in his books, shows and life events. For his endless love and dedication to all of us. You literally saved my life.

I'm most grateful to the Divine for preserving and guiding me on the path to a better existence, leading me to suitable teachers, books and materials that helped me move forward, for being by my side, protecting me and my loved ones.

I'm grateful for every small occurrence that has helped me be here and now, accepting and loving myself as I am!

Much of love and let it be light!

Printed in the United States
by Baker & Taylor Publisher Services